FAN-TASTIC SPORTING STORIES!

FAN -TASTIC

SPORTING STORIES!

GRAHAM SHARPE

300 TRUE TALES OF FANS WHO STOLE THE SPOTLIGHT

The Robson Press

First published in Great Britain in 2013 by
The Robson Press (an imprint of Biteback Publishing Ltd)
Westminster Tower
3 Albert Embankment
London SE1 7SP
Copyright © Graham Sharpe 2013

Front cover images: Scottish fans at Wembley (l) and Erika Roe (r)
© Press Association; Eric Cantona © Rex Features

ISBN 978-1-84954-599-0

10 9 8 7 6 5 4 3 2 1

A CIP catalogue record for this book is available from the British Library.

Set in Sabon

Printed and bound in Great Britain by
CPI Group (UK) Ltd, Croydon CR0 4YY

MIX
Paper from
responsible sources
FSC   FSC® C020471
www.fsc.org

To Charlie Walker, fellow Wealdstone FC and racing fan, a pal from way back who was always there until, shockingly, he no longer was.

INTRODUCTION

We may not all be participants in sport, but most of us are quite happy to take part vicariously, giving advice and criticism from the sidelines, enjoying what's going on if it is going our way, moaning, ranting or raving a bit if it isn't. That is generally the full extent of our input. We rarely contemplate becoming more involved in the event ourselves, becoming part of the action, even influencing the outcome, or creating a situation in which the fan becomes the story.

'Fan' – of course, the word is commonly used to describe a supporter or follower of various sporting events. But where did this usage come from?

Most, if asked for an opinion, would probably suggest it has become an accepted abbreviation of the word 'fanatic', originally from the Latin 'fanaticus', meaning 'insanely but divinely inspired', illustrating a rather extreme form of interest in something, above and beyond that of the usual casual viewer.

Another suggestion, which is rather intriguing, is put forward by Graeme Kent in his book *Boxing Shorts*, where he tells of his suspicion that the term 'is derived from the "Fancy", the name given to the aristocratic backers of the early prize ring'.

But those early days are so long ago – back in the eighteenth century – that it is more than possible that the already well-used description was lazily applied to the followers, aristocratic or otherwise, of other sports as they were invented.

The reasons that people become fans, and in particular sports fans, have been studied by psychologists such as Dan Wann at Kentucky's Murray State University, one of four authors of *Sports Fans: The Psychology and Social Impact of Spectators*.

Wann and his fellow scholars attribute people becoming fans to a number of factors: one element is entertainment, because sports spectatorship is a form of leisure. But sport is also a form of escapism, and being a fan provides an excuse to shout and rant at something and/ or someone, an activity that may be constrained in other areas of one's life.

Fan activities offer participants a combination of euphoria and stress (usually about the potential for their team to lose) for which the word 'eustress' was coined. Fans experience euphoria during moments when play is going well for their team, and stress when play is going against their team. This tension between the two emotions generates an unusual sense of pleasure or heightened sensations.

Wann also points out that those not involved in sport as fans often 'hold a negative view of sports fans and spectators. They perceive them as beer-drinking couch potatoes, with a pathological obsession with a trivial and socially disruptive activity.'

I'm pleased to tell you that this is the type of fan you'll find well represented in this collection.

Very few of us live up to the fanatical aspect of being a fan. As Patrick Collins of the *Mail on Sunday* put it in a December 2012 column about fans in sport, we usually 'recognise the convention by which the watchers watch and the performers perform'.

But not all do. And these are the rare animals this book will introduce you to, from the benign to the malign. From the wonderful Erika Roe to the loathsome Aaron Crawley; from the barely believable Michael O'Brien, to the literally incredible James Jarrett Miller.

All they have in common is that they should not have been part of an event but somehow imposed their presence on the spectacle and either enhanced or traduced it.

We've all seen this happen, I'm sure. I remember being at the Swiss Derby at a racecourse near Zurich when one of the runners broke loose and ran a couple of circuits of the track watched by thousands, all of us wondering when he'd tire and slow down to be caught.

One race fan wasn't prepared to wait for that to happen. He swaggered slowly and ostentatiously down to the rails, ducked under them, waited patiently for the runaway colt to head back in front of the stands, raised his hands confidently to stop him – and was promptly mown down as the horse sped up, trampled over him and set off for another circuit, leaving the local medics to rush over with a stretcher on which our battered, bruised and bleeding wannabe hero was carried off…

I mentioned Erika Roe – those of, er, a certain age will be aware of the impact of this young lady who decided to enliven the action during a rugby union international between England and Australia. I was at the game, which was played at Twickenham, when Ms Roe made her bid for immortality. I'd already been staggered by the different attitude between opposing supporters at rugby, compared with football. Having ended up alongside some hefty Aussie fans, I'd feared the worst when I trod on the toes of one particularly burly specimen during an exciting passage of play – only to have my breath taken away, not by an Antipodean punch, but by his apology for getting in my way. As for Ms Roe – well, she brightened up a dull afternoon by stripping off and streaking across the pitch; although I was at the opposite end, where we had to stand on tiptoe and crick our necks to see past the idiot dancing in front of us dressed as a gorilla in order to glimpse Erika in all her glory...

The pal I had gone to the game with, John Maule, a Brit turned Aussie, told me of another fan intervention incident he had witnessed: 'I was on the hill at the Sydney Cricket Ground when they put a piglet over the fence, wearing a little Botham jumper – he took some catching!'

One of the earliest examples of a fan finding himself making as much news as the sport he was following occurred in 1882, when Australia beat England by seven runs at the Oval – the match which would lead to the inauguration of the Ashes phenomenon – and an England fan was so overcome by the excitement of the whole thing that he suffered a heart attack and perished.

Even earlier than this, it is recorded that Roman Emperor Theodosius had to abandon the Olympic Games of 393 AD when spectator riots broke out after Greek athletes alleged that Roman competitors were professionals.

The previously mentioned *Mail on Sunday* writer Patrick Collins's *Among the Fans* was short-listed for the prestigious William Hill Sports Book of the Year Award. The excellent volume dealt with several sports, including tennis, cricket, speedway, greyhound racing, darts, rugby, golf and snooker, with Collins defining fans as 'people who make our sports both possible and pleasurable' and asking, 'What are they doing there? How do they behave? Are they there to see or be seen?'

Fellow sports writer, Roger Alton, executive editor at *The Times*, also proffered a plausible explanation for foul football fan behaviour in October 2012: 'Once footballers started being paid obscene salaries ... it broke the link with communities and warped any sense of duty and responsibility. Players and managers now seem to operate (with) little concept of responsibility, and the moral boundaries of barbarians. And this sets an example to the fans.'

In this book we will be looking at the fans who are very much there to be seen, heard or even to participate in the event and by doing so influence what is happening on the pitch, track, court or in the arena.

When they do so as individuals, the outcome is sometimes unpredictable, but usually relatively easily contained.

But when groups, gangs or mobs of fans form, their influence over the outcome of an event or even on whether it actually takes place or plays out to a conclusion is often of a malign nature.

It is difficult ever to imagine a time when sportspeople

would pay to encourage fans to support them, but for all that, major sporting events would be pointless without fans – and the presence of supporters, spectators, fans is essential to create the atmosphere from which the sportspeople feed.

Although he clearly did not like it, Rafa Benitez, then Chelsea's interim manager, was clearly suffering from the effects of the fans' opinion of him when he let rip at them in February 2013 after he had seen his side win at Middlesbrough in the FA Cup.

A large contingent of Chelsea fans had made their antipathy towards the appointment of Benitez obvious since his arrival and virtually every game was marked by booing and singing of anti-Rafa songs.

He bore it stoically until snapping and letting his true feelings come out, which is very unusual as most bosses are well aware that once they 'lose' the fans the risk of losing their job increases exponentially. This time, though, the fans had got to the boss – which, of course, is the ultimate objective of such behaviour.

However, Benitez got off lightly: in October 2013, fans of Levski Sofia stormed a press conference held to unveil new boss Ivaylo Petev, whom they believed to be a supporter of rivals CSKA. Petev was stripped of his club top and forced out of the room. He resigned.

With the ever escalating cost of admission to major sporting events one can envisage fans eventually being priced out of the market – but without them, watching televised events would be much diminished.

So perhaps the inevitable consequence of rising prices and fan disillusionment will be computer-generated crowds for TV sport – and then the days of fan misbehaviour will be well and truly over!

But for now, let us delve into the long tradition of fan madness that has enriched sporting experience since balls were first kicked, racquets swung, and races contested...

GREAT COACHING

After suffering a 3–2 defeat at the hands of Accrington Stanley in 2012–13, and facing up to potential relegation, it can hardly have been a jolly journey for Barnet's die-hard devotees on the 200-plus-mile drive home – and the thirty-six fans on the supporters' club coach felt even worse when they broke down on the M6.

But help was at hand from an unlikely source – Dutch player-manager Edgar Davids.

When the Barnet team's bus spotted the stranded fans shivering on the hard shoulder waiting for a replacement coach, Davids ordered the driver to stop at the next service station and told his players to disembark.

The former Champions League winner, who had earlier been red-carded, then sent the team bus back up the M6 to collect the Barnet fans and bring them to the service station, where he bought them coffee while they waited for their transport home to be repaired.

MORT-IFIED

A grandmother was banned from supporting her village rugby club for 'loutish behaviour'. A passionate fan of Pyle Rugby Club, near Bridgend, South Wales, for more than fifty years, Lillian Mort, seventy-four, brought her team into disrepute with her frequent foul language and abusive outbursts directed at the unfortunate referee. When her behaviour earned the club a £50 fine in March 2013, enough was enough, and they barred Mort from watching the side for three months. Not to be put off, the pensioner took to watching matches through the steel railings around the field.

BORUC HAS BOTTLE

Southampton keeper Artur Boruc said racist abuse from his own fans resulted in him throwing a water bottle at them during a match in 2012. It happened on his home debut against Tottenham Hotspur as the Saints went down 2–1. The club took no action after Boruc told them, 'I won't say I regret it, because I heard insults from the stands. Racist ones.'

DEADLY SHOOT-OUT

Who knew that watching a penalty shoot-out can kill fans? That's what was claimed in 2000 by researchers at the University Medical Centre in Utrecht, Holland, after they looked at deaths on the day in June 1996 when the Dutch were beaten on penalties by France, thus being knocked out of the European Championships. They compared death rates with the five days before and after the match, and compared the same period with other years.

Deaths from heart attacks or strokes in men, but not women, rose 50 per cent.

In the *British Medical Journal*, Prof. Diedrick Grobbee said that unusual mental or emotional stress and high alcohol consumption are recognised triggers for strokes and heart attacks. However, suicide as a result of sporting event is rare. But the death of a thirty-year-old man who fell 65ft at the Atlanta Braves' Turner Field baseball park in August 2013, during a rain delay in a game, was ruled a suicide by the Medical Examiner's Office.

TASTY BURGERS

Fans of German side Hamburger SV received a unique gesture from their club following their 9–2 defeat to Bundesliga leaders Bayern Munich on Saturday 30 March 2013.

As an apology to supporters who had had to endure the drubbing, the club invited fans to a barbecue at their training centre, all paid for by the players.

Any hamburgers on the menu, one wonders?

BADLY LET DOWN?

Lifelong Cleveland Browns fan Scott E. Entsminger left one final request for the somewhat unsuccessful club he had followed for so long when he passed away aged fifty-five in Ohio in July 2013.

In an obituary published in his local newspaper, Mr Entsminger's last wish was quoted: 'He respectfully requests six Cleveland Browns pallbearers…'

However, his request to the American football club carried a sting in the tail: '…so the Browns can let him down one last time.'

The Browns are not noted for their triumphs these days – their last NFL Championship was gained in 1964, and among supporters their First Energy stadium is known not as the 'Theatre of Dreams' but as the 'Factory of Sadness'.

Unsurprisingly enough, the club was not keen to go along with Scott's dying wish, but to show they bore him no ill feeling, they presented his family with a team shirt bearing the name of his favourite player, Lou Graza.

ALL TOO TRAGIC

It reads like the script for a violent Hollywood horror movie, but the events played out during a football match in Brazil in June 2013 were apparently all too true.

The game was taking place at a ground in the state of Maranhão in north-east Brazil, and the flashpoint began after referee Otavia Jordão da Silva, 20, sent off player Josenir Abreu, 30.

The red card resulted in official and player becoming involved in a fist fight – at which point, according to a report by the Press Association, Mr Silva 'took out a knife and stabbed Mr Abreu, who died on his way to hospital'.

At this point, fans watching the game 'rushed into the field, stoned the referee to death and quartered his body'.

Local media reports alleged that the spectators also

decapitated the arbiter 'and stuck the referee's head on a stake in the middle of the football field'.

Police reportedly later arrested a 27-year-old suspect. Police chief Valter Costa was quoted as saying, 'One crime will never justify another.'

FAN JUMPS TO IT

Roger Federer was leading 6–1, 2–1 against Sweden's Robin Söderling at the 2009 French Open when, as Federer prepared to serve, a spectator dressed in red and white and brandishing a Barcelona FC flag climbed over the courtside wall, rushed up to him – and tried to place a red hat on his head.

Security guards chased the fan, who ran off before eventually being brought down and carried from the court.

As he was being taken away he was heard claiming that he had wanted to pay homage to Federer and make a gesture against dethroned Spanish champion Rafael Nadal, a fan of Barcelona's arch-rivals Real Madrid.

Federer, who still managed to win the match, remembered that it had not been the first time such an incident had happened to him during a match, recalling similar intrusions at Wimbledon and Montreal.

'I didn't know what had happened until I heard the crowd react,' he said. 'So that gave me a fright seeing him so close right away. Normally they look at you and say "sorry, I have to do this", but this guy looked at me and I was not sure what he wanted. He seemed to want to give me something. It was a touch scary.'

The fan was revealed to be a serial intruder at sporting events, going by the name of Jimmy Jump (real name Jaume Marquet i Cot), who boasts his own self-promotional website on which he sells T-shirts with his own logo on it.

His dedication to the Barcelona cause has taken him far and wide. During the UEFA Euro 2004 final between Greece and Portugal in Lisbon, he threw a Barcelona flag at the Portuguese captain, Luís Figo, who had left that team to join Real Madrid four years earlier. He has invaded the pitch at Champions League, Euro and World Cup semi-finals and finals in England, Switzerland, South Africa and Hungary, to name just a few.

Not a man to limit himself, Jump doesn't confine his appearances to Barcelona-related events. During the 2006 Champions League semi-final between Villareal and Arsenal, he ran onto the pitch just before the second half began. When on the pitch, he tossed a Barcelona jersey at Arsenal striker Thierry Henry, with Henry's name and number 14 printed on the back. (On 25 June

2007, Henry was transferred to Barcelona from Arsenal and given his lucky number 14.) Jimmy was apprehended and taken into custody by stadium security, and later fined by Spain's anti-violence commission.

Another one of his 'raids' was at the end of the Euro 2008 semi-final match between Germany and Turkey in Basel, Switzerland; this time he had a Tibetan flag and wore a T-shirt with the slogan 'Tibet is not China'.

Nor indeed does Jimmy restrict himself to disrupting football games. He ran through the starting grid during the parade lap of the 2004 Spanish Grand Prix; entered the court during a basketball game between Memphis Grizzlies and FC Barcelona Bàsquet, attempting to confront a player; and invaded the pitch at the start of the second half of the 2007 Rugby World Cup final between England and South Africa.

He is also one of the few pitch invaders, fans or streakers to interrupt a water polo game, making his aquatic debut when he jumped into the CN Sant Andreu pool during the 2010 Copa del Rey final between CN Sabadell and CN Barcelona.

In 2012, his friend and Irish musician Rob Smith (who is also a well-known fan of Barcelona) wrote and recorded a song about him called 'Salta Salta (The Jimmy Jump Song)', which featured a small part of Barcelona FC's anthem 'El Cant del Barça' during the outro.

PEAR STOPS PLAY

A Swedish league football match was abandoned after a player was hit in the stomach by a pear.

Gbenga Arokoyo, a Mjällby defender, doubled up in pain after being hit by the flying fruit as he and his teammates celebrated a goal at Djurgården's home stadium in Stockholm in April 2013.

The game was called off as a hail of bottles, coins and fruit was hurled at players by the home fans.

FANS SUPPORT WITH PRIDE

The Chicago Cubs flew the flag for Gay Pride when they hosted nearly 350 gay and lesbian fans for the Cubs' game against the Los Angeles Dodgers in August 2013. A feature of Out at Wrigley, the largest LGBT-attended major league sports event, the game marked the thirteenth year in a row that the Cubs had taken on hosting duties for the event.

Laura Ricketts, Chicago Cubs co-owner, board member and Chicago Cubs Charities chair, said before the game: 'We're immensely proud to be flying the Pride flag above Wrigley field.'

Ricketts became the first openly gay Major League

Baseball owner when her family took ownership of the Cubs from the Tribune Company in 2009.

'The LGBT community happens to be a big part of the Cubs community. We have a lot of LGBT fans and, of course, it's important to me personally because I happen to be a part of the LGBT community,' said Ricketts. 'Owning a team itself is a bit surreal and a big responsibility, but I feel an even greater responsibility because I'm a woman, an out woman. For me it's an incredible source of pride and it's very humbling.'

TALEFANS

Brazilian football champions Fluminense intervened when, in an apparent excess of fighting spirit, fans launched the 'Be a Taliban Warrior' campaign. Disgusted with their team's loss in a Copa Libertadores match, the Fluminense fans had taken to Twitter to ask players and fans to take and post photographs of themselves dressed as Taliban fighters to 'show their warrior spirit'.

Several players, among them Brazil striker Fred, posted photos with their faces partially covered by scarves in club colours, while some Brazilian fans started turning up to matches carrying flags depicting controversial figures such as Ayatollah Khomeini, Saddam Hussein and Osama bin Laden in the colours of their clubs.

But with Brazil preparing to host the 2014 World Cup, the football authorities were beginning to fear that the fans' attitude could damage the country's image. In a statement, they denounced the campaign, which they said would only glorify terrorism.

The statement read: 'The intentions of those who began this movement and have joined it clash with the Taliban's image, who are terrorists and not healthy warriors.'

The club described the 'Be a Taliban Warrior' campaign as a 'call for violence'.

PHIL-THY HABIT

A spectator who spat at sixteen-time World Champion Phil Taylor during a Premier League darts match in Glasgow in March 2013 was immediately banned by the sport's governing body.

Taylor had been walking to the stage to take on Raymond van Barneveld and expressed his 'disgust' at being hit on the ear when a fan spat at him. 'I wanted to give the fans a show, so it is a shame if one tries to spoil it,' said Taylor. Darts chief Barry Hearn said, 'It was disgraceful, cowardly behaviour – the guy was ejected immediately and won't be back to watch darts. There were 8,000 people there but you always get the odd idiot.'

RED-FACED RIDE

Liverpool defender Martin Skrtel was the victim of fan fury in March 2008. Having jumped into a cab in Liverpool and asked to be taken home, the Slovak defender was stunned to be thrown out of the taxi by the cabbie, who told him he was an Everton fan!

POWERFUL FAN

Notorious trickster Karl Power from Droylsden, Manchester, gained himself a reputation as a true fanatic when he began inveigling his way into sporting events by pretending to be a player. He first came to attention when he appeared in the Manchester United team photo before a UEFA Champions League match against Bayern Munich in 2001.

Power gained access to the pitch by pretending to be

with a TV crew, then took his place in the stands again afterwards to watch the game.

When the England cricket team played against Australia at Headingley in 2001, Power walked out to bat with the team. Moments after entering the field, he removed his helmet and was immediately recognised.

At Silverstone in 2002, he beat Michael Schumacher to the winners' podium at the British Grand Prix.

Power managed to get onto Centre Court at Wimbledon in 2002 and began to hit balls to an accomplice, Tommy Dun, prior to a Tim Henman match.

On 5 April 2003, Power and several friends invaded the Old Trafford pitch ahead of Manchester United's game with Liverpool. Dressed in full United kit, Power and company re-enacted a goal scored by Diego Forlán against Liverpool at Anfield earlier that season.

Following this stunt Power was banned for life by Manchester United.

YOU'RE KIDDING...

A band of young cricket fans found themselves the centre of unexpected attention when they started an impromptu match among themselves during a rain break at the third Ashes Test match at Old Trafford in August 2013.

Shortly after play commenced behind a stand at Old Trafford, the young amateurs were warned by stewards to stop on 'health and safety' grounds.

But their supporters weren't standing for it: hundreds of adult fans backed them up, showing their disapproval by chanting 'Are you Aussies in disguise?' at the heavy-handed officials.

'People were singing at the stewards,' said BBC journalist Ian Shoesmith, who was among those watching the game.

He said one adult fan was ejected from the ground for bowling at one of the children during their game.

'People were telling them, "This is ridiculous – Old Trafford is a home of cricket",' said Mr Shoesmith. 'Eventually a club official in a suit came up to them and told them to turn a blind eye.'

FANTASY GIRL

Fans of American football star Manti Te'o, playing for Indiana's Notre Dame University, were 'heartbroken' to hear that the player's girlfriend was dying from leukaemia. And even more so when they discovered that not only was she not dying, but that she didn't really exist at all!

After Te'o took his team to sporting victory on the very evening of his girlfriend's funeral, his story made national news. Te'o gave a series of interviews telling how his grief had spurred him on to victory, and the inspirational tale was held up as an example of achievement in the face of adversity. But when the media investigated further, they discovered that his so-called soulmate, 'Lennay Kekua', had never existed.

According to Te'o's team, the 21-year-old had been 'duped into an online relationship' with a woman whose illness was 'faked by perpetrators of an elaborate hoax'.

FANS IN A FINE MESS

A sneaky sheriff used match day to good effect when he spent the time investigating the cars parked outside an August 2013 Aussie Rules game at Melbourne Cricket Ground between Collingwood and Essendon.

In total, twenty-seven cars were found to have fines attached to their registrations, including speeding tickets and parking infringements, when Victorian sheriff Brendan Facey used an automatic number plate recognition system to detect offenders at the game, attended by 68,821 people.

One driver, reportedly owing almost AUD$26,000,

had his car clamped and Sheriff Facey said 'there was a very stern conversation had before the car could be returned'.

Mr Facey said it was an 'honourable draw' between Essendon and Collingwood supporters for outstanding fines.

BANKING ON IT

After being charged with robbing twenty-four California banks during 1991, Claude Dawson Jones admitted that he had pulled off the raids in order to finance his trips to watch his favourite American football team, the Los Angeles, er, Raiders.

RALLY UNUSUAL

Not a sport one might associate with fan skulduggery, perhaps, but the 1994 RAC Rally was rocked by allegations of chicanery designed to help land a British win, which was eventually achieved by Scotland's Colin McRae.

During the final day of the competition, two tree trunks were placed across the path of contender Carlos Sainz of

Spain – and when he duly went into a ditch, the spectators who came to help somehow took all of thirty minutes to haul the car and driver out, drawing a wry comment from former winner Juha Kankkunen that 'a lot of people were trying to help – but I'm not sure how hard'.

ICE-SCALATING VIOLENCE

It started with the suspension of top Montreal Canadiens ice hockey player Maurice Richard, after he whacked a match official over the head with his stick – and ended with a full-scale fan riot with looting, a blaze and millions of dollars' worth of damage as fans' protests about Richard's suspension at the end of the 1954–55 season got somewhat out of hand.

DIVORCED FOR BEING A FAN

A woman identified only by the name Rowley brought her marriage to an end in 1981 on the grounds that her husband was too big a fan of cricket to be a good husband.

She told Wolverhampton Divorce Court that she had initiated the proceedings on the basis of her other half's 'excessive obsession with cricket, both participatively and statistically'.

The court accepted the claim and permitted the divorce.

SINKING FEELING

'The friends of competitors sometimes manoeuvred large boats or barges into their opponents' paths or positioned themselves on bridges over the racecourse in order to drop heavy stones into their opponents' boats as they passed underneath.'

– Author Daniel James Brown, in his 2013 book *The Boys in the Boat*, on eighteenth-century boat races among London watermen on the Thames, in which unscrupulous fans helped out their favourite crew.

FAN INVASION

When England played Scotland on 6 April 1891, the game took place at Blackburn Rovers' Ewood Park ground, with the home side prevailing narrowly by 2–1.

But when the local paper, the *Northern Daily*

Telegraph, wrote about the match, they were more concerned with the crowd than the result – and, in particular, with the activities of the visiting Scotland fans. Interestingly enough, local football fans were not that concerned with the match as they were still smarting from the fact that no members of the Rovers side, which had recently won the FA Cup, had been deemed good enough to play for the nation, and the majority of the 10,000 crowd was from north of the border.

As the *Northern Daily* put it,

It is estimated that about 5,000 men travelled by the excursion from Glasgow and Edinburgh and they commenced to arrive as early as four o'clock in the morning.

Soon after this hour, sleeping townsmen were alarmed by shrieking war whoops and riotous singing, accompanied in several places with the crash of glass and smash of door panels.

One tradesman in a principal street on drawing aside his blind to see the occasion of the blood-curdling tumult, was startled to perceive a 'braw Scot' perched on the top of the pole supporting one end of his sun-blind, and coolly smoking a cigar; while another gentleman was making vigorous efforts to climb up the other standard.

In King William Street a stubbornly contested football

game was in full swing before six o'clock, every kick being signalised by a perfect storm of howls and shrieks.

Scores of householders found drunken men asleep in their doorways and passages when they came down to breakfast. Long before dinner time drunken men were staggering about the streets in all directions, and the accommodation afforded by the police cells was tested to the bursting point.

Soon after midday, the majority of the visitors went off to Ewood Park to witness the match, and the remarkable spectacle was witnessed by scores of Scotchmen, in all stages of intoxication, sprawling on the seats of the stands, either asleep or sleepily quarrelsome.

The return train got away at about midnight after indescribable scenes, many of the passengers having to make distressing spurts to cover the distance between police stations and the railway in the short time allowed them by the guardians of the peace. Large numbers never caught the trains at all.

FANS WITH HEARTS IN THE RIGHT PLACE

In August 2013, a group of Hearts fans with an interest in the side's links to the First World War uncovered long-standing debts owed by the club to the Lady

Haig Poppy Factory ... and settled them out of their own pockets.

Papers from the club's administrators showed that Hearts owed £185 to the poppy factory for wreaths bought before the Tynecastle side went into administration. But officers from McCrae's Battalion Trust reportedly paid over £400, the extra sum covering wreaths which had been ordered in advance, never to be delivered.

The trust commemorates the 16th Royal Scots, which suffered heavy losses during the First World War, with casualties numbering many football players from Hearts and other Scottish clubs, including Raith Rovers and Dunfermline.

Antony Kozlowski, officer of McCrae's Battalion Trust, said that he and colleagues had decided to settle the debt with their own money, as it would not be appropriate for the trust to foot the bill. 'We stepped in because we knew that nobody else could by law.'

GOLF FANS PIN PLAYERS DOWN

Golf fans were recently offered the unique opportunity of having a say in a major tournament's pin placement. Over 92,000 fans voted for one of the four offered placements of the fifteenth hole on the final day of the 2013 US PGA, being held at the Oak Hill Country Club.

And with commendable lack of concern for the dignity of the players, they voted for the most difficult of the placements for the 175-yard par three – to the back right of the green, four yards from the right edge, twenty-five yards from the front.

'Miss the green and it's bye-bye golf ball. Miss left and the golfer might not be able to stop their chip from going into the drink,' wrote *USA Today* sportswriter Kevin Oklobzija.

Voting took place via a website, Twitter and Facebook, and player reaction seemed positive, with Graeme McDowell tweeting to encourage people to vote – 'We require a lot more fan interaction than we have' – while Zach Johnson added, 'Any way we can incorporate the fans is good.'

ALMOND A RUGBY NUT?

Watching a sporting event at which H. H. Almond was a spectator must have been an extraordinary affair.

The nineteenth-century schoolmaster, who reigned over activities at Edinburgh's Loretto educational establishment from 1862 to 1902, was reportedly incapable of watching any sporting contest without becoming outrageously exercised.

Author David Randall said of him, 'His excitement when watching even a junior house football match reached such a violent pitch that in later life he had to be restrained by force from spectating lest a seizure overwhelm him.'

Hely Hutchinson Almond, who attended Balliol College, Oxford, was among those responsible for introducing the game of rugby into the Edinburgh area of Scotland.

ANTI-FAN

The Rev. Samuel Ashe was a late-eighteenth-century English clergyman based in Langley Burrell in Wiltshire, who objected to sport being played on the Sabbath, so used to spend his Sunday afternoons hiding in the trees by the local sports field.

He would bide his time until a ball came near him, when he would catch any errant football or rugby ball and pierce its bladder with a large pin. He could then go home rejoicing that he had stopped his parishioners from sinning.

However, sinners they may have been, but they

weren't about to stand for such treatment and soon took to bringing an extra ball with them, thus leaving the Rev. ashen-faced as his efforts were scuppered.

MARIA BROWN-ED OFF?

Brian and Susan Brown from Wolverhampton were keen boxing fans.

So keen that when they had a daughter in April 1974 they decided to name her Maria Brown.

But not only Maria – her middle names were Sullivan Corbett Fitzsimmons Jeffries Hart Burns Johnson Willard Dempsey Tunney Schmeling Sharkey Carnera Baer Braddock Louis Charles Walcott Marciano Patterson Johansson Liston Clay Frazier Foreman – a real heavyweight selection.

HIGH DRAMA

Tranmere's match against Mansfield in April 2003 was abandoned 'for safety reasons' after a supporter, who was later charged, climbed high above the heads of the crowd up a floodlight and then onto the roof of the 'Cow' stand – and refused point-blank to come down.

With Tranmere winning 2–0, the referee decided the game could not continue at half-time and the 7,000 fans had to leave the ground while police endeavoured to talk the man down, which they managed after the best part of half an hour. If he was a disgruntled Mansfield fan, his actions achieved nothing as results elsewhere meant they were relegated.

The incident had echoes of a time when, during the 1920s, Watford's then Cassio Road ground used to be so packed that fans used to watch from nearby tree-tops. One regular was Joey Goodchild, who would jump onto the main stand roof and entertain those inside and out with a display of tap dancing.

However, at one game Joey lost his balance and tripped and fell on to a man and a woman below. The man had his glasses broken and the woman later won £25 compensation from the club. Joey was barred from returning to the roof.

DOWNHILL ALL THE WAY

As drivers Vincenzo Lancia and Felice Nazzaro battled it out in their Fiats to win the 1900 Padua–Treviso race, contested over 136 miles, both were disqualified 'because spectators pushed them up a hill'.

DRAC-DELLER

Keith Deller knew his life was about to change when he won the 1983 Embassy World Professional Darts Championship – but he didn't think it might involve joining the undead into the bargain. However, one of his fans apparently did, for she wrote to him explaining that she thought when he smiled he 'looked just like Dracula'.

Oh, and she wondered whether 'you would like to sink your teeth into my neck?'

It was an offer Deller was able to ignore – as, I imagine, did tennis star John Lloyd when he received mail from a male fan requesting that Lloyd should wear a headband on his next visit to the tennis court, as a signal to his correspondent that 'it would be all right to come to his hotel room after the match'.

The golfer Sandy Lyle also once received an offer he could refuse through the post, when, having been selected to play in the USA for Britain's Walker Cup team, an elderly gentleman sent him a cheque, suggesting he might use it to buy himself 'chewing gum and chocolate' while he was in the States.

Flamboyant 1960s British wrestler Adrian Street had gathered fans galore with his colourful and unusual-for-the-times appearance – but even he was surprised when an airmail envelope arrived from Germany, containing within a proposition from his fans in a Hamburg brothel, who were extending an 'open invitation' to visit the ladies of the house and sample their wares for free.

Soccer boss Lawrie McMenemy was on good terms with his postman, who, he said, brought him plenty of fan mail: 'I get lots of letters from women – between the ages of 80 and 100. My wife has no problems on that score.'

John McEnroe's postbag once contained a gift from a Japanese fan, a doll of himself, which was immediately grabbed by his then girlfriend, Stacey Margolin, who installed it at the side of her Beverly Hills bed – and used it as a punch-bag every time Mac irritated her in some way, which was a not uncommon occurrence.

NUN OF THAT

When Holland scored against Argentina in the 1978 World Cup final, a truck driver who shouted 'hooray!' attracted the attentions of Sister Collette Duveen, a nun from the Order of Merciful Sisters who, for reasons best known to herself, then took it on herself, as it was reported at the time, to 'kick in the teeth' of the shocked – and now toothless – man.

FED-UP FAN

John Robinson was a loyal West Ham fan who turned up for a 1975 game hoping to see his heroes triumph. Unfortunately, those fans behind John in the turnstile queue as he prepared to enter the stadium soon realised they could be in for quite a weight – sorry, wait.

For John, who tipped the scales at 35½ stone and was proud of his status as Britain's second heaviest man, had become jammed in the innards of the turnstile.

He could neither move forward nor retreat backwards. He was well and truly stuck in the no man's land between entrance and exit. As the situation began to look likely to last past kick-off time, drastic action was called for and with the assistance of 'four blokes' who pushed and shoved, John was finally able to get into the ground.

'I usually go to the games in my platform heel shoes, which leaves ample room for my stomach to clear the turnstile,' he said later. 'But I kept my working boots on and got stuck.'

TATTOO TOO MUCH?

Andy Murray's historic 2013 Wimbledon triumph sparked a rush to the tattoo parlours by delighted fans.

First off the block and under the ink was 41-year-old father of three Richie Callaghan from Broomhall, Edinburgh, who endured a three-hour session with tattooist Paul Slifer in his Red Hot + Blue Tattoo establishment, who waived his usual four-month waiting list as he was so enthused by the opportunity of honouring Andy.

The result was a large, striking image of Andy kissing his Wimbledon trophy, now forever gracing the left-hand side of Callaghan's chest, just above his nipple.

'I chose the picture because you can see how much lifting that cup meant to him.'

Craig Gourlay, a 28-year-old painter and decorator from Glasgow, decided to have his own leg decorated with a Wimbledon badge along with a thistle, Andy's name and the date – duly delivered by 26-year-old Clydebank woman Megan Wilson of Black Pearl Tattoos, who confirmed that Andy tattoos had become 'a very popular idea'.

HOGETTE THE LIMELIGHT

No strangers to attention, a group of Washington Redskins fans made a reputation for themselves by turning up to games attired in women's dresses, garden party hats, and pig snouts – as you do! Calling themselves The Hogettes, this band of superfans, founded in 1983, were spurred on not only by their love of the team but by their urge to raise money for charity.

Over the course of their fan-tastic career, which spanned almost thirty years, the posse managed to raise a whopping $100 million for charitable causes, including Children's Miracle Network, Ronald McDonald House, and March of Dimes. When they announced their retirement at the end of 2012, they numbered twelve active and fifteen former members, including three inducted into the Pro Football Hall of Fame as part of the VISA Hall of Fans.

BAILING OUT THE CLIPPERS

Meet Darrell Bailey – or, as he's better known, Clipper Darrell. Hailed by the *New York Times* as the 'unofficial biggest fan' of the NBA's Los Angeles Clippers, Darrell began his superfan career under somewhat inauspicious circumstances. In 1984, when being fired from his job as an electrician, our hero was told he would 'never amount to anything'. Not long after, he heard an announcer say exactly the same thing about the Clippers – and so a fan was born.

Labouring under the name 'Dancing Man' for his initial appearances, Bailey soon changed to the moniker

'Clipper Darrell', racking up a score of 386 consecutive appearances before his streak was ended by a hospital visit to treat his high blood pressure.

His act includes dancing, cheerleading and – above all – taunting the opposing team at home games, all while decked in the Clippers' team colours, red and blue. Among his repertoire of chants are the upbeat 'Let's go, Clippers!' and the rather more severe 'U-G-L-Y, you ain't got no alibi, you ugly!' – the latter usually directed at opposing players when they shoot free throws.

And his colour scheme isn't limited to his clothes: Bailey, a married father of four, drives a customised 1995 BMW 740i with red, white and blue throughout both exterior and interior. His home, meanwhile, is also painted in the team's colours, with a red, white and blue basketball court in the driveway and a Clippers logo on the pavement. The front door is red and the living room is white and blue with Clippers logos prominent from the walls to the floor tiles.

Surprised he didn't open a 'Clipper' joint!

A SMALL CHOICE

Willie Crilley – known by fans, inevitably, as 'Wee', due to his short stature – was a 5ft 1in. forward who, in the 1921–22 season, hit forty-nine League goals in the

Scottish Second Division for Alloa, whose other players managed just thirty-two between them.

But his love affair with the fans was cemented when, in a game against King's Park, Crilley found a way past the defenders and was left with just the keeper to beat – at which point he stopped and indicated to the supporters to decide which corner of the goal he should score in – and duly did as they requested.

GIVING CLUB THE BIRD

With his club in a financial crisis just two years into their existence, one Sunderland fan decided in 1881 that he must make the ultimate sacrifice to help ensure their survival.

So he sold off his prize canary – along with its cage – in a raffle raising what was then the decent amount of one pound, which was then handed over to grateful club officials.

BEER BATTERED

Laurie Lee made his name with his 1959 book *Cider with Rosie* – but Lee found himself affected by a different kind of alcohol when he attended a cricket match in Sydney. The British author was felled and rendered unconscious by a beer bottle flung by one of the famously rowdy occupants of the 'Hill' area of Sydney Cricket Ground.

'If I go back I'll wear a tin hat,' commented Lee on coming round.

NET LOSS

Desperate to stop fights being disrupted by rowdy French fans, promoter Jeff Dickson, active in Paris after the First World War, came up with the idea of suspending a heavy meshed net over the ring, in order to be able to lower it if necessary to stop the bottles, coins and other objects that were being flung into the ring from endangering the fighters.

Sure enough, when the atmosphere became somewhat heated during one thrilling scrap, down came the net, which duly prevented missiles reaching the ring – but also left the pugilists and the crowd in the dark and unable to see much.

The 'net result' was that the solution caused too many problems and was promptly ditched.

TOUGH FOR TAFFS

Following complaints from Welsh fans that they had been arrested for no apparent reason while in Paris to see their side take on France in the 1985 Five Nations tournament, a forthright French *gendarme* spokesman admitted to newspaper *Le Figaro* that in fact they were right on the money – explaining that it was 'so that they could go home and tell their friends what to expect'.

DEAD CERT

Racing fan Alan Rix of Truro, Cornwall, brought new meaning to the phrase 'die-hard fan', managing to show his appreciation for the sport even after shuffling off this mortal coil. When the 62-year-old died in May 1989, he was cremated in a coffin containing betting slips and a copy of the *Sporting Life* racing newspaper – then his ashes were scattered at Newton Abbot racecourse.

FASHION STATEMENT

The scene: New York's Madison Square Garden. The occasion: the New York Knicks playing the Toronto

Raptors one Monday evening in March 2003. The stars: the Knicks' small forward Latrell Sprewell ... and Calvin Klein.

Apparently mistaking the court for a catwalk, the world-famous fashion designer couldn't contain himself during the game, and left his courtside seat to strike up a conversation with the Knicks star just as Sprewell was about to make a play.

Klein caught Sprewell by the arm and tried to engage him in conversation – although Sprewell later said he couldn't understand what sixty-year-old Klein was saying or asking him.

'I wasn't nervous. I was a little surprised, like, "Is security going to come over here at some point or what?" I didn't know that was him.'

Klein was eventually escorted back to his seat, but with his ardour seemingly undiminished – as he sat back down he let out a cry of 'Sprewell!'

OH, BABE

After being ejected from a May 1922 game at the Polo Grounds in New York City for throwing dirt in the eyes of the umpire, baseball legend Babe Ruth chased a heckler through the stands.

When the fan outpaced the pursuing superstar, the raging Ruth returned to the dugout roof and challenged any fan in attendance to fight him – 'Come on down and fight! Anyone who wants to fight, come down on the field! Ah, you're all alike, you're all yellow!'

Ruth was suspended for seven games and fined $200 for the incident.

NASTY PROTEST

Taking part in the 1982 Dutch Open, the always volatile Romanian tennis star Ilie Nastase became upset with a linesman who had ruled against him on a crucial point.

Rather than take it out on the linesman, Nastase, usually a crowd favourite, registered his outrage by grabbing a vendor's load of ice cream cones and hurling some at fans.

He then returned to the court, daubed the linesman with ice cream, and played on as though nothing had happened.

BELLE STRIKES

Albert Belle, who disliked being called by his nickname, 'Joey', was in the Cleveland Stadium outfield during a

1991 game when fan Jeff Pillar yelled to him from the stands, 'Hey, Joey, keg party at my place after the game, c'mon over.'

That might seem to have been a friendly enough invitation, unlikely to prompt any adverse response.

But at the time, it was a virulent jibe, as Belle had spent much of the previous summer in an alcohol rehab programme.

Belle promptly picked up a foul ball and threw a perfect strike at Pillar's chest from about 15 feet away, leaving the fan with a weltering souvenir.

Belle had the clear support of the fans for his action, and they gave him a round of applause for nailing the heckler, though he was later suspended and fined.

KINN YOU BELIEVE IT!

Long-time Cardiff fan and former leader of the Labour Party Lord Neil Kinnock appeared to have forgotten his manners while watching a Premier League football match at Fulham's Craven Cottage ground in September 2013.

He was sitting among home supporters in the Ernie Clay Stand when his team scored the opening goal of the game in the twelfth minute, and was unable to contain his glee.

Most regular football followers are well aware that to celebrate audibly and/or visibly while in the midst of supporters of the opposite team is poor form at best, tantamount to a suicide note at worst. Not, it seems, Lord K, 71, who made his delight that Cardiff had taken the lead only too obvious to the Fulham fans around him.

They, not to labour the point, despite being famous for their mild manners and bonhomie, did not take too kindly to this infiltrator demonstrating his approval of the goal their team had just conceded.

A quick-thinking steward intervened and politely 'suggested' the Kinnock party may wish to relocate to a different part of the ground, where they would be able to mingle with like-minded Cardiff fans.

They made a strategic withdrawal – 'coincidentally' just after the goal was scored, according to a later comment from a Kinnock spokesperson.

However, it appears likely that even from his place with the away supporters his reaction when Cardiff clinched the game with another goal deep into added time could be heard and enjoyed by every member of the Fulham faithful.

The Labour peer had previously been quoted as saying, 'Decorum will not come into it if Cardiff win.'

THAT'LL SHOE HIM

Boston Bruins players rushed to the defence of their teammates Stan Jonathan and Terry O'Reilly when the former was hit across the face with a rolled-up programme and the latter's stick was stolen at the end of a December 1979 ice hockey game between the New York Rangers and the Boston Bruins at Madison Square Garden. Jonathan and O'Reilly's stalwart colleagues climbed into the stands to show their displeasure, tussling with the opposition fans.

Defence player Mike Milbury particularly distinguished himself in the brawl, removing a fan's shoe and beating him with it.

The game ended with four Rangers fans in police custody, O'Reilly suspended for eight games, Milbury and Peter McNab suspended for six games apiece, and all three sportsmen fined $500.

FATAL DECISION

A riot broke out at the Nabire Regency Boxing Championship in Indonesia in July 2013 when the final scores came in.

The points awarded by a panel of judges were to decide the championship match for the Bupati Cup, and when the judges had made their decision, it seemed it wasn't to everyone's taste. The losing boxer's supporters began throwing chairs at the judges, and the winner's supporters responded by throwing bottles and broken chairs, panicking people in the stadium.

Police and soldiers were deployed to stop the fighting, but as about 1,500 spectators scrambled out from the two working exits, a stampede ensued which left some eighteen fans dead – most of them women trampled in the rush – and forty injured.

WHACK'S GOING ON?

'Jerome Simpson came off the side-line and whacked the guy,' said the commentator during the Minnesota Vikings' match against San Francisco 49ers.

A routine comment in American football matches – but the difference this time was that Simpson had 'whacked' one of two fans who had come onto the pitch during the August 2013 game.

'Simpson roughed up the guy a little bit,' elaborated Al Michaels.

The game resumed once the two interlopers were removed, only for another to enter the playing area later on – but the players stayed out of the way on that occasion.

FAN-TASTIC QUOTES

'Footes Lane with 1,000+ home fans is home advantage. Do not clap opposition goals!'

– Guernsey FC club captain Sam Cochrane, taking to Twitter in August 2013 in an effort to discourage fans of the club, now in the national pyramid system, from being so fair to their opponents. 'Supporters far too nice. Make our home a tough away fixture,' urged Cochrane.

'Fans, treated shamefully as cattle in the '70s and '80s, are now largely cash cows for milking in the twenty-first century.'

– Henry Winter of the *Sunday Telegraph*, 20 January 2013.

'A sporting, impartial gallery will inspire players on court, while an ignorant one, favouring one side, can often spoil a match. Never applaud a difficult "get" in the middle of the rally, this is apt to make a player miss his next stroke unnecessarily. The decisions of the umpire or linesman should never be questioned from the stands. These officials are in a better position to judge.'

– Advice to fans attending Wimbledon from the *Daily Express*, 20 June 1927.

'At too many clubs there is too little respect for supporters; lip service for the "twelfth man" concept when it appeals, but otherwise it is "take, take, take and if you don't pay up then we'll find some other mug who will".'

– *The Times*'s chief football correspondent, Oliver Kay, 21 January 2013.

'This was just a very small boo, and stars are always booed, so I'm a star, you have to take it this way.'

– The answer of FIFA President Sepp Blatter to a question about being booed by fans during the Olympics, as reported by Paul Kelso of the *Daily Telegraph*, 14 January 2013. Of course you do, Sepp, you old star.

'They've paid 62 quid over there, go and see them.'

– Reported comments of assistant ref John Brooks to Manchester City players after a January 2013 game against Arsenal at the Emirates, suggesting they should acknowledge their fans, who had travelled such a distance and paid so much to see them play. He was stood down from his future appointments for his trouble!

'The natural state of the football fan is bitter disappointment, no matter what the score.'

    – Clearly a man after my own heart, writer and Arsenal fan Nick Hornby from his 1992 William Hill Sports Book of the Year winner, *Fever Pitch*.

'It's as if the crowd don't just watch – they're part of the race. They're close enough to touch as you pass and the children love to slap hands and high-five with the runners. The smallest stretch their tiny arms upwards and glow with delight if you dip to touch their fingers.'

    – Lifelong athlete and author of *The London Marathon* John Bryant on the essence of fandom as it enhances the capital's great once-a-year spectacle.

GOLFERS FAN OUT

The golf fan who insisted on shouting as soon as Ian Poulter had played a shot during the US PGA Championship in August 2013 did not impress the British player, who suggested giving the players weapons with which to silence irritating spectators. 'We should be allowed to take 10,000-volt tasers onto the course and taser every muppet who shouts out something stupid,' ranted Poulter. He was not the only player lashing out at fans, a number of whom had recently taken to replacing the irritating 'You the man!' and 'Get in the hole!' with the totally inane 'Mashed potatoes!'

Lee Westwood joined in the fan fun after his six-over-par round of 76 ended his chances of winning the tournament, and with it his first major. When he was criticised by fans on Twitter, Westwood hit straight back, tweeting, 'Will you get a life?' then calling the fans 'a***holes sat behind a keyboard with a pitiful life'.

As the Twitter spat continued, Westwood apparently thought he'd gone too far and tweeted that he was not having a go at 'decent human beings, followers' but 'just the p****s that should be locked up by the Twitter police'.

He had to go even further later on, offering 'sincere

apologies to my sponsors and true followers for my earlier comments'.

And Poulter's public complaints merely resulted in more of the same clamour from the fans at his next tournament.

Racing Post editor Bruce Millington suggested, 'Burly security guards should prowl the fairways on the look-out for these oafs, and eject them the moment they open their traps.' I presume he was referring to the fans, not the players!

RAINBOW ROLLEN

Rollen Stewart fascinated and repulsed TV directors and viewers in equal measure when he began to pop up on screens in the late 1970s and 1980s, usually at golf tournaments but also at other major sporting events, where he had a knack of finding himself just in shot, sporting an eye-catching rainbow wig and holding a sign reading 'John 3:16'. The message referred to a passage in the Bible reading, 'For God so loved the world, that he gave his only begotten son, that whosoever believeth in him should not perish, but have everlasting life.'

With his bushy beard and sideburns, Stewart, aka Rock 'n' Rollen, aka Rainbow Man, also landed a role in a Budweiser TV advert and was even the subject of a *Saturday Night Live* sketch.

Born in 1944, he became a fixture at a wide range of sporting contests, trying to spread the Biblical word, but embarked on an enforced absence from the sporting scene when, in the early 1990s, he was jailed for life following a hostage situation in a California hotel.

RAFA FLARE-UP

Rafael Nadal has seen most things on a tennis court during his record-breaking career – but even he was left nonplussed after a literal fan flare-up during his eighth victory in nine attempts at the French Open in June 2013.

Rafa was cruising to a straightforward three-set win over David Ferrer when, suddenly, a smoking flare was thrown onto the court by a half-naked, masked fan who made it onto the court and began to move in Rafas's direction before being hustled away. It transpired he had been making a protest against the same-sex marriage laws recently put in place in France.

Minutes earlier, other fans had made a loud, but short-lived protest about children's rights.

Nadal continued serenely to win 6–3, 6–2, 6–3.

MOST ILL-JUDGED FAN COMPLAINT?

Manchester United fan Peter Molyneux was at the end of his tether at the poor form being shown by his club. So much so that he decided to make a banner on which to register his dissatisfaction at the performance of the club boss.

It was December 1989 and Molyneux duly crafted the banner, using paint from his shed and a bed sheet. He took the banner along to the home game against Crystal Palace. 'THREE YEARS OF EXCUSES AND IT'S STILL CRAP', it read, attracting a good number of approving glances and verbal agreement.

Pete and his banner were at Old Trafford, Manchester United's home ground – and also on the banner was the name of the current manager, with an appropriate fare-well message added – 'TA RA, FERGIE'.

Yes, Pete was launching an 'Alex Ferguson out' campaign. Perhaps the worst-judged effort to remove a club manager in the history of the game!

Twenty-three years later, Pete unveiled another banner at Old Trafford on the day Sir Alex retired – this time it said, '23 YEARS OF SILVERWARE AND WE'RE STILL TOP: TA RA, FERGIE'.

Not only that, the fan then wrote a book entitled *Ta Ra Fergie*, published in 2013, chronicling his fifty years of following the club since 1963 – with the banner featuring prominently on the front cover.

BULL-YING FANS

One of the least-expected examples of fans being involved in fatalities I have come across in research for this volume concerns bullfighting.

Timothy Mitchell is a writer on bullfighting whose books include *Blood Sport: A Social History of Spanish Bullfighting*, and he records that 'the impulsive evaluations of bullfight crowds rattle and unnerve bullfighters, sometimes leading them to commit acts that result in serious injury or death'.

Mitchell cites a 1920 crowd of fans 'hounding [matador] Joselito into fatal temerity at Talavera', and another in 1947 that 'drove Manolete to impale himself on the horns of Islero'. And in 1981, he writes, at the Almeria Fair, 'the normally cautious Curro Romero was gored in an attempt to appease a hastily judgemental crowd'.

He adds that a famous bullfighting novel by Blasco Ibanez ends with this description of fans: 'The beast roared: the real one, the only one.'

RE-MARCK-ABLE

Feyenoord players applauded fan Rooie Marck as the terminally ill 54-year-old was stretchered onto the pitch on a bed decked out in club colours in July 2013.

It was Marck's dying wish to meet the players, and the club made it happen on their first training day, the day when they traditionally invite fans in to see the squad prepare for the season to come.

Fellow fans in the De Kuip stadium had created a banner honouring Marck and sang 'You'll Never Walk Alone' in emotional scenes. Marck even conducted a chant of 'Feyenoord till I die'.

Cancer-stricken Marck passed away three days later.

FAN'S BALLPARK FIGURE

In 2006, an anonymous cricket fan paid £26,400 for the ball Garry Sobers had hammered over the boundary at Swansea during his record-breaking over of six sixes against Glamorgan bowler Malcolm Nash in August 1968.

Sobers was playing for Nottinghamshire and when the ball, now signed by him, came up for sale in November 2006, it was bought at auction at Christie's.

However, doubts were raised about the authenticity of the ball when cricket writer Grahame Lloyd discovered that the high-earning ball was made by Duke & Son, whereas the one bowled had – according to the bowler – been a 'Stuart Sturridge' brand.

Later claims that more than one ball was used during the over did nothing to help solve the mystery, and when the ball was due to come up for auction again in May 2012, it was withdrawn before the sale could take place.

Lloyd, who had spent eighteen months investigating the provenance of the ball, called for the original purchaser to be reimbursed.

FANS ABANDON GAME

Fans of top Greek league side AEK Athens invaded the pitch in the eighty-seventh minute of their game at home to relegation rivals Panthrakikos in April 2013, forcing the abandonment of the game they were losing 0–1.

It was unclear whether the fans were trying to ensure the game was replayed in order to give them a chance of winning the points, or whether they were intent on doing damage to the players, who they blamed for putting them into relegation trouble.

AEK were subsequently relegated for the first time in their history as the points for a 0–3 win were awarded to their visitors.

PRESIDENTIAL PRESSURE

The fan who grabbed a stadium announcer's microphone and began to abuse the referee was no ordinary spectator.

FC Terek Grozny were being held to a goalless draw by FC Rubin Kazan in their Russian Premier League game in March 2013 when, with just four minutes remaining, Ramzan Kadyrov could contain his frustration no longer and, to huge applause from fellow fans, launched his verbal tirade against referee Mikhail Vilkhov, who had red-carded one of his side's players and failed to award what had looked to be a cast-iron penalty.

'The referee is corrupt,' he shouted, adding one or two personal insults – 'Sell-out! … Donkey!' – for good luck.

His outburst did not inspire his side to win or the ref to give them a penalty.

'The game was just awful because of the biased referee,' declared the fan after the match on social media. 'The groundless second yellow for Utsiev, the penalty that wasn't given – he did everything to change the course of the game.' And who was Ramzan Kadyrov? Not only the chairman of the club, but also leader of the Chechen Republic, who has been accused by human rights activists of a number of rather unpleasant activities off the pitch.

When questioned about his pitchside outburst, Kadyrov wasn't covering anything up. 'Yes, it was I,' he admitted unrepentantly. 'I had good reasons.'

He refused to apologise and there are no reports of the referee pushing the matter any further…

ARE KU JOKING?

Another high-profile fan to attempt to interfere with a ref's authority during an important match was Sheikh Fahad Al-Ahmad Al-Sabah, head of the Kuwaiti FA.

With Kuwait trailing 3–1 to France during their 1982 World Cup finals match, their players stopped in their tracks when they heard the ref blow his whistle.

The French carried on, scoring a fourth, to the despair of the Kuwaitis, as it became obvious that the whistle was not blown on the pitch.

The referee was oblivious to Kuwait's protestations and told them to kick off.

At this point, the sheikh entered the picture, striding out onto the pitch and remonstrating with the startled official, who promptly changed his decision and instead awarded a drop-ball restart and ruled out the goal.

The sheikh was subsequently fined a derisory $10,000.

The ref never officiated at another international game.

BOXER HITS BACK AT FAN

The boxing fan abusing fighter Curtis Woodhouse on Twitter after his defeat in an English title bout to Shayne Singleton in March 2013 little dreamed that he would find the irate pugilist turning up at his house.

But the posting online by someone dubbing themselves 'the master' so upset Woodhouse that he decided to track whoever it was down and confront him.

Not only did he find his tormentor, he drove to his home and tweeted a picture of the man's street sign to his own 18,000 followers.

'right Jimbob im here!!!!' tweeted Woodhouse as he closed in on his prey, asking his followers to 'tell me what number he lives at, or do I have to knock on any door'.

Cowering at home, the fan, later named as Sheffield man James O'Brien, 24, was forced into an abject apology, tweeting 'i am sorry its getting abit [*sic*] out of hand I am in the wrong I accept that.'

Woodhouse, who was a former professional footballer with Birmingham and Sheffield United said, 'I thought, "I'm not taking this." If somebody was saying those things to me in the street I couldn't just walk past. So I spoke to some people who knew some people. I know who he is now … when he realised I was outside his house he started squirming.'

STU-PENDOUS FAN

When 67-year-old Stuart Astill was told by his doctor that the operation he had just undergone on his foot meant he would not be able to travel to Burnley from his Derbyshire home in April 2013, he was philosophical about it.

Of course, the retired British Rail engineer was disappointed at having to miss his team, Nottingham Forest, play at Burnley in a Championship match. But then, he could afford to miss one – after all, he had watched Forest 1,786 times in the previous forty years without ever missing a game!

The first time he ever watched them was as long ago as 1956. 'I knew my run had to end at some point,' said Stuart.

SHAKEN, NOT STIRRED

The internet video meme known as the 'Harlem Shake', which became an online phenomenon in 2012, resulted in tens of thousands of performances by many individuals and organisations watched by millions all over the world. But it had started out in life when a New York basketball fan called Albert Boyce, aka Al B, created it to entertain fellow fans.

Albert started his impromptu half-time performances in the Entertainer's Basketball Classic tournament matches he attended in Harlem, at Rucker Park in the early 1980s. 'He would dance and twist his shoulders,' explained Albert's mother Sandra, whose son died in 2006, aged forty-three.

Al B's moves struck a chord with fans at the matches and soon spread more widely, eventually going viral, and on 22 May 2012, Bauer released the song 'Harlem Shake', creating the worldwide craze which rivalled even Psy's 'Gangnam Style' song and dance.

WRESTLING WITH HIS CONSCIENCE

Okay, we all know the clue to the WWE is in the 'Entertainment' part of its title, but if you were a fan determined to gatecrash a sporting event, would you choose to do so by attacking a wrestler?

Even if you were confident their 'fights' are scripted in advance, they are still pretty hefty guys, more than capable of looking after themselves.

But that did not deter one gentleman who attended a WWE show in South Africa at the end of July 2013.

With star wrestler Randy Orton – 6ft 5in. tall, apparently, and pretty sturdy with it – standing in the ring, he was suddenly attacked by a fan, who jumped up onto the canvas and hit him with a low blow.

The interloper, reportedly the first of his type, was hustled away and presumably arrested.

The WWE even issued an official statement about the incident, another reason to believe it was genuine:

WWE.com has learned that Randy Orton was violently attacked by an audience member during a SmackDown World Tour Live Event in Cape Town, South Africa, Tuesday evening. Footage of the attack was captured by a WWE fan and posted to YouTube, and shows the perpetrator striking The Viper from behind. Orton reportedly suffered an injured groin in the attack but is well enough to have performed Wednesday night in South Africa.

They added two days later:

The accused party pleaded guilty in court yesterday, August 1, 2013, and was charged and ordered to either pay a fine of 500 Rand or, alternatively, serve 30 days in jail.

After acknowledging his wrongfulness, the accused individual was given a three-year suspended sentence, and is not permitted to attend WWE's Live Events in Johannesburg, South Africa, this week.

Some reports suggested the perpetrator of the attack was himself a wrestler, and the incident did spark a social media discussion about whether it was a genuine attack or not – a legacy of the years of outrageous stunted incidents which have taken place in televised wrestling.

TELL SID

For the best part of fifty years, one racing fan has divided opinion among French 'turfistes'.

Sidney – or, sometimes, Sydney – makes regular appearances at many different racecourses, often in and around Paris, and takes up a position in the parade ring or at the prize-giving, treating fellow racegoers to a variety of opinions and observations.

He is regarded by the majority as an entertaining if occasionally irritating presence, who enhances the scene, which, in the absence of bookmakers on French tracks, can become a little quiet between races.

However, Si(y)dney's appearance at Saint-Cloud race-course during 2012 provoked the racecourse manager there, Hugues Girard, to crack and demand that he should 'pipe down' and keep his opinions to himself.

The target of this verbal attack was duly affronted: 'I was instructed to shut up. I replied that we were not in a hospital nor a cemetery, but a public place. I've been to racetracks for fifty years, even the horses recognise me, no one is going to shut me up...'

And Si(y)dney was supported by a leading Paris trainer, Jean Paul Gallorini: 'Sidney is part of our sport's lifeblood, he's part of the institution, something we'll all be aware of until the day he's no longer here.'

An online racing fan, calling him- or herself 'Moonage', posted the following comment:

Sydney has been a feature of Parisien [*sic*] racetracks for over thirty years. He can be found at Auteuil, Longchamp, Vincennes etc., etc. He is always surrounded by an avid following of people looking for tips. He sings (even in English if there are any present), he engages with those around him (but never in an aggressive way), he congratulates, he asks for tips (albeit politely and fairly discreetly) and several times I've seen professionals (i.e. jockeys & trainers) cross the parade ring to talk to him.

All racegoers know him, and only novices/newcomers are surprised by his behaviour. Sydney is a well-established institution who goes way back, and people worry about him when he's not around. I understand he can also be found at boxing matches.

Another poster, 'Kaiku', recalled that 'Sydney' was at the Arc for Alleged's first win in 1977.

There was an exchange of views about him in the comments section of a website on racing for national broadcaster RTL, where one user wrote:

I've seen several racegoers on here eulogise about a certain Sydney. This isn't the view held by everyone, even the majority of racegoers, who are fed up of this individual who tends to ruin things a bit.

Many professionals are annoyed by his stupid and untimely outbursts and can't wait to get away from him.

You'll have no trouble finding him, he plonks himself in front of any TV camera about to make sure he's seen as much as possible. For me, he's just another 'Did you see me?' and I have to wonder how he can just wander in to the weighing room at Vincennes like he owns the place. This is just my view although I have a fair few friends who agree.

But another, anonymous, racegoer hit back:

'My recollections of "Sydney" go back as far as the '80s, if he's still about today, well, I for one say "all the better"! Must one be part of the elite to enjoy a day at the races?'

Joe (aka Jolyon) Williams, who runs the excellent Chateau Racing company from his base in Chateaubriand, and supplied many of the details in this piece, told me: 'I also found a story about a famous French crooner, Michel Sardou, going to Vincennes recently to watch his trotter run and happily posing for a picture with the aforementioned Sydney.'

It appears that the jury is still, after half a century, out on the question of Si(y)d's negative or positive contribution to the racing scene in France. A little like racing fans still cannot agree on John McCririck's value to the British turf.

LIP SERVICE

Athletics fan Kathrine Switzer was annoyed that women were not permitted to enter the annual Boston Marathon.

But when she checked the race rules there was nothing specifically preventing them from doing so – so she entered as K. V. Switzer.

As the 1967 race was about to get under way the German-born Switzer set off, wearing number 261. After four miles she was chased by race official Jock Semple, who was determined to throw her out of the event, shouting 'Get the hell out of my race' at her and even grabbing hold of her at one point.

Boyfriend Tom Miller was not surprised that Kathrine was noticed early on, having told her beforehand, 'Take off the lipstick – somebody might see you are a girl and not let you run.'

But Kathrine never went anywhere without her lipstick and wasn't about to start doing so now!

Lipstick or not, she finished the race in 4 hours 20 minutes, commenting, 'I was just a kid who wanted to run her first marathon.'

Ironically, Kathrine was beaten by another female fan who took part in the race unofficially, Bobbi Gibb.

Despite Kathrine's actions it was five years before women were officially allowed to enter the race.

CAERPHILLY DOES IT, GEOFF

Geoff Huish was arguing with pals at the Leigh Social Club in Caerphilly, South Wales, prior to the Six Nations match between England and Wales in early 2005.

The 29-year-old Wales fan Geoff declared pessimistically to friend Gethin Probert, 'If Wales win, I'll cut my balls off.'

His mates laughed off the remark but after Wales won the game 11–9, Huish returned home – where he duly severed his testicles, returning to the club wearing a kilt and holding the removed objects in a bag.

Staff dialled 999 and put the testicles in a pint glass filled with ice cubes.

An ambulance arrived, and Huish was soon in hospital suffering from severe blood loss, facing up to the possibility of being fitted with a prosthetic scrotum.

A fan who was with Geoff at Leigh Social Club in Caerphilly said, 'He lifted the kilt up to show everyone what he had done. There was blood everywhere, it was terrible. That's when he collapsed.'

Geoffrey revealed two years later in an interview with *The Sun* that he 'took an agonising ten minutes to perform the horrific op using a pair of blunt wire cutters' and that afterwards he had fished the testicles out of the toilet.

FAN AS MAN OF MATCH?

Very few fans have actually managed to take part in a competitive game and influence the outcome themselves with their actions during the contest, but with the November 1961 American football match between the Dallas Texans and Boston Patriots delicately poised and time running out, a play was taking place as a Boston fan actually came onto the pitch and interfered with a pass which could have prevented his side's 28–21 victory.

It was a bizarre ending as the raincoat-clad man knocked down a potential game-tying touchdown from Cotton Davidson to Chris Burford on the game's final play.

Incredibly, the play was allowed to stand and Boston won. No one seems ever to have identified the guilty fan.

You'll find footage on YouTube.

SNOW GOOD COMPLAINING

Snowy weather didn't make for a winter wonderland for the Oakland Raiders when they played the Denver Broncos in November 1999. After spending much of the second half being pelted with snowballs, the Raiders' Charles Woodson finally retaliated. Unfortunately, the snowball he threw back into the crowd managed to hit a female fan in the face.

An arrest warrant was later issued for Woodson – and nor was he the only one to find himself on thin ice. A drunken Broncos fan who had been throwing snowballs at the Raiders' tackle Lincoln Kennedy was ejected from the stadium – but only after Kennedy had run into the stands and punched him square in the face.

Winter weather had caused similar sporting chaos for the San Diego Chargers in their game against the New York Giants at Giants Stadium in December 1995. With the Chargers 27–17 ahead during the fourth quarter, intoxicated Giants fans threw hundreds of snowballs and chunks of ice at opposition players and team officials, injuring fifteen people, while Chargers equipment manager Sid Brooks was knocked unconscious and stretchered off. There were fifteen arrests and a further 175 people were ejected, with seventy-five fans later having their season tickets withdrawn.

ALIVE AND KICKING

Many's the fan who's been given a stadium ban over the years, but such petty penalties weren't stopping one die-hard fan during the 2011–12 KNVB Cup between Eredivisie clubs Ajax and AZ Alkmaar at Amsterdam Arena. In the thirty-sixth minute of a fourth-round match, Ajax held a 1–0 lead when our fanatic ran onto the pitch and launched a karate kick from behind at AZ goalkeeper Esteban Alvarado, who managed to kick back several times before security arrived and arrested his assailant.

When Alvarado was sent off for retaliating against his attacker, AZ walked off the pitch and the match was abandoned.

The KNVB later rescinded the red card and ordered the match to be replayed in its entirety behind closed doors. As for that stadium ban, our unnamed fan saw his three-year ban upped to a whopping thirty years – and was then hit with a lifetime ban from the club and its season ticket list. The club itself was fined €10,000 for failing to prevent him from entering the pitch, and given a suspended one-match spectator ban (not including the replay).

SEAT OF POWER

Sunderland AFC moved to standing room only on Boxing Day 2012: fans arrived at the Stadium of Light to find a number of seats firmly taped up, bearing notes reading, 'This season card has been suspended due to persistent standing.' According to club officials, standing had become such a problem that they could, er, stand it no longer.

They reported an 'increasing number of complaints' from fans who were infuriated that their view was being spoiled by their fellow spectators refusing to sit down. To combat the problem, they suspended a record number of fans from using their season tickets for the game: thirty-eight in total, compared to just twenty during the whole of the previous season.

KNEE-SY THING TO DO

During the Fourth Test in Pakistan during December 1980, West Indies star Sylvester Clarke was pelted with oranges and stones by spectators while fielding on the boundary.

He responded by picking up a nearby brick and hurling it into the crowd, badly injuring a spectator who later required emergency surgery. A riot was narrowly averted only when Clarke's quick-thinking teammate Alvin Kallicharran went down on bended knee to apologise to the crowd.

Reflecting wryly on the incident many years later, England cricketer Phil Edmonds wrote that the brick 'probably swung in late and viciously before hitting him on the head'. Clarke was suspended from the team for three matches for his actions.

THAT'S PANTS

The *Sun* newspaper reported in December 2012 that nineteen-year-old Birmingham City fan Rory Coates had been banned from matches for three years and fined £200 after taking a smoke bomb to a match against local rivals Wolverhampton Wanderers – hidden in his underpants.

OSMOND KIL-ER BLOW

In February 2013, the world made a surprising discovery: Marie Osmond had become a Kilmarnock FC fan!

The BBC reported that she had visited the club's home ground to give a rendering of her most famous song, 'Paper Roses', bizarrely adopted by the club's supporters, to 500 specially invited season ticket holders.

HOW'S THAT?

Those who think fan-based brawls are a modern problem, perhaps even a symptom of a recent decline in moral values, might want to look away now: the Sydney Riot of February 1879 proved our forefathers could more than match our rowdy behaviour. The fracas involved up to 2,000 fans, who took the pitch by storm after an umpiring dispute broke out between members of the visiting English cricket team and the New South Wales Cricket Association.

But despite the grand scale of this scene of fan participation, records suggest only three arrests were made.

I BEG YOUR PARDON?

Galatasaray fans were declared the loudest in the world, reported the *Daily Mail* in February 2013, as the home crowd at the Turk Telekom Arena recorded a sound level of 131 decibels at a recent derby match – louder than standing 50 metres away from a military jet taking off and louder even than an infamous 1976 gig by rockers The Who, which only reached 126 decibels.

BUSHWHACKED

During a match at the 1991 Wimbledon tournament between Stefan Edberg and John McEnroe, a fan claiming to be the US President, George H. W. Bush, jumped onto the scoreboard, briefly interrupting play.

After he was removed from the court, a steward commented, 'He was completely out to lunch.'

JOCK-ULAR OUTCOME

Both runners in a January 1920 Plumpton Novice Chase fell. Amerongen was remounted to win, while Longerline came in second thanks to the efforts of a spectator who caught and rode the other horse in himself. As Mr Dale made the weight, his placing in second was officially recognised.

FAN-WAY PARK

A fan at Fenway Park, home of the Boston Red Sox baseball team, started a ruckus when he took a swing at New York Yankees' Gary Sheffield as the right-fielder was fielding a ball in play during an April 2005 game. Roused, Sheffield took a swing back at the fan, but in the meantime another spectator had decided to join the fray. The newcomer threw beer at Sheffield, then jumped back, tripping over the fan next to him.

Ever the professional, Sheffield threw the ball back into the infield before approaching the fan who had launched the attack. What might have happened next is anyone's guess – but, perhaps luckily, security intervened.

The fan was ejected from the stadium and had his season tickets revoked.

HEDGING YOUR BETS

A report in the *Market Rasen Mail* following their race day on Easter Monday, 24 April 1905, reveals that a racegoer, one Mr Cottingham, 'had accidentally been jumped upon (whether by competitor or mounted spectator I do not know)' and that he was 'recovering in the Cottage Hospital at Market Rasen'.

The report says he had been 'sheltering' behind the hedge.

As you do.

FIERY FAMILY OF FANS

Sporting passion seems to have lit a spark in two fans, William Thomas and his eleven-year-old son, during an April 1976 baseball game. The pair ran into the outfield at Dodger Stadium, trying to set fire to an American flag with matches and lighter fluid.

Chicago Cubs player Rick Monday grabbed the flag and carried it away to a standing ovation. Dodgers coach Tommy Lasorda ran out and launched a profanity-filled tirade at the protesters before being restrained by security.

Thomas and his son were arrested, though their motives were never revealed.

BOXING MATCH BLOW

Running at Fontwell in May 1995, the eight-year-old horse Boxing Match acquired a unique form book entry: 'Weakening when hit streaker, pulled up.'

A 29-year-old spectator, Stephen Brighton, had disrobed at the trackside and run onto the course – straight into the path of Boxing Match and his rider, Rodney Farrant.

NOT SO PROUD OF FANS

A particularly bad-tempered Victoria Football League Aussie Rules match came to a violent conclusion in June 1908 when a group of Fitzroy fans could contain themselves no longer. Invading the ground at the Brunswick

Street Oval after the game against Essendon, the enraged Fitzroyites launched an assault on rival players as they tried to leave the field, forcing Essendon fans to jump the fence in order to protect their players.

In the mêlée that ensued, players, fans and even team officials piled in: Essendon's captain Alan Belcher ended up being escorted from the ground under the protection of Victoria police constable and former Collingwood player Bill Proudfoot.

TOUR DE FAN-CE

Fan antics left a lasting impression on the Tour de France in 1904 after supporters of a local favourite took their partisanship a step too far. Die-hard devotees of Antoine Fauré physically attacked several of their hero's opponents as the riders neared the peak of the Col de la République in the Loire. It was 1950 before the Tour route returned to the region.

FLARE UP

Romanian soccer saw fireworks in October 2011 when a Liga I game between FC Petrolul Ploieşti and FC

Steaua Bucureşti wasn't going Petrolul's way. The referee's decision to award a penalty kick to Steaua evidently went down poorly with Dragos Petrut Enache, because the crazed Petrolul fan – who was later found to be on drugs – ran onto the field and launched an attack on Steaua defender George Galamaz, hitting him in the face with a heavy object. Galamaz suffered a broken cheekbone and temporary loss of hearing.

His teammates retaliated on his behalf, Novak Martinović and Răzvan Stanca launching themselves on Enache and landing several kicks before security arrived on the scene. Both players received red cards. When play resumed, Steaua converted the penalty kick to go 2–0 up, at which point Petrolul fans began throwing flares onto the field. When Steaua goalkeeper Ciprian Tătăruşanu was injured by one of the flares, the referee decided enough was enough, and the game was abandoned. Enache was arrested and jailed.

UGLY INCIDENT

The *Observer* newspaper reported in October 2012 that Argentinian model Cinthia Fernandez, who had gone to see her boyfriend Matias Defederico playing for his club Huracan, took such exception to a fan calling him 'rubbish' that she not only swore at the vocal spectator but also administered a sound beating.

She later commented: 'I thank all the nice people who intervened. This was an ugly affair.'

WHY DON'T U F.O.?

Fan Gigi Boni called a halt to a soccer match between Fiorentina reserves and Pistoiese in October 1954 – because he spotted UFOs, or flying saucers as they were called then, swooping over the pitch.

Officials stopped the game while players and fans watched 'the incredible sight'. Gigi said later, 'They were moving very fast and then they just stopped. It lasted a couple of minutes – I would describe them as being like Cuban cigars.'

CAWL OF THE WILD

Leeds fan Aaron Cawley gave a near-perfect illustration of the term 'football hooligan' during a Championship game in October 2012 – and earned himself a jail sentence into the bargain. Evidently not a man to do things by halves, Cawley had been drinking heavily before he arrived at the match between his beloved Leeds and their opponents Sheffield Wednesday: he claimed to have drunk several cans of strong lager, three-quarters of a litre of vodka, and seven to ten pints of cider before the game. And the alcohol had clearly done little for his temperament, as Sheffield Wednesday keeper Chris Kirkland discovered to his cost when the belligerent fan ran out onto the pitch at Hillsborough and attacked him.

Kirkland required medical attention following the assault, which saw him being struck in the face by the 21-year-old fan.

At his court hearing, Cawley, from Cheltenham, Gloucestershire, pleaded guilty to assault and entering the field. He was given a sixteen-week jail sentence and a lengthy football banning order to add to his rap sheet – along with the two previous banning orders he'd already breached.

Cawley emailed the police to say sorry and also emailed Sky Sports, who broadcast the match, in the hope that his apology would be passed on to Kirkland and both clubs.

But despite his remorse, his team weren't having him back. A spokesman for Leeds United said, 'The club will ban the individual for life from Elland Road when this banning order expires. While we are pleased to see justice brought so quickly, our one disappointment is that we feel the sentence could, and should, have been considerably longer.'

YANKS VERY MUCH

New York Yankees teenage fan Sal Durante caught the record sixty-first home run ball hammered into the crowd by batter Roger Maris in October 1961 – and was told by the hitter, who had just erased the legendary Babe Ruth from the record books, that he could keep the ball as a souvenir. He did so, later selling it for a reported $5,000 to a California restaurant owner who promptly gave the ball to Maris.

Durante was even invited to the club to join in the fiftieth anniversary celebrations of the feat in 2011.

PREMIERSHIP IN A STATE

The 1967 Tasmanian State Premiership Grand Final between Wynyard and North Hobart ended in uproar as North Hobart's David Collins went back to take a kick after the siren with Wynyard leading by one point. Hundreds of Wynyard fans watching the game at West

Park in Burnie invaded the field, tearing down goalposts in a bid to stop the full-forward taking his kick.

Despite the best efforts of umpires, players, team officials and police to clear a path for Collins, he eventually had to be escorted from the ground under police protection. And nor was that the extent of the injury suffered: Collins's teammate Barry Styles was left unconscious with broken fingers after being trampled by the crowd and had to be carried from the field on a stretcher.

The Tasmanian Football League declared the Grand Final a 'no result' and withheld the 1967 State Premiership.

WEDDED TO THE TEAM

Freeman Reese and his late wife Betty were such fans of the Alabama college football team that when they were told by their daughter that she was to be married, Freeman warned her to set the date with care. 'We told her, just don't get married on a game day and we'll be there, 100 per cent, and she went off and picked the third Saturday in October, which everybody knows is when Alabama plays Tennessee, so we told her, hey, we got a ball game to go to.'

It may or may not be a saving grace that the Reeses did condescend to drive from the game to attend the reception.

LIFETIME VAN

Alcohol, that old scourge of many a sports event, was at work once again during a Tri-Nations rugby match in Durban in August 2002. Partway through the game between South Africa and New Zealand, Pieter van Zyl, a South African fan who had been enjoying more than a bit of the hard stuff, scaled a perimeter fence, ran onto the pitch and tackled the referee, David McHugh of Ireland. McHugh came out of the incident with a dislocated shoulder, and had to be carried from the pitch on a stretcher. But van Zyl didn't escape unscathed either: All Blacks flanker Richie McCaw promptly punched him in the face and wrestled him to the ground, where he kept the fan until police and security arrived on the scene. When all was resolved, van Zyl was left with a conviction for trespassing and assault, a sentence of three months in jail, a fine of $275 and a lifetime ban from attending rugby matches in South Africa.

GUNNING FOR THEM

With five minutes of extra time left in a 1936 Olympic football match between Peru and Austria, a number of Peruvian fans, one brandishing a revolver, invaded the pitch and assaulted Austrian players, officials and stadium security.

During the confusion, Peru scored twice and 'won' the match 4–2. The IOC and FIFA, perhaps unsurprisingly, declared the game null and void, and ordered a replay two days later behind closed doors. Peru, however, refused to play the rerun and withdrew from the Games. Austria, declared winners by default, went on to win the silver medal.

FLAGGING PROTEST

During the gold-medal match in the women's table tennis between China's Deng Yaping and Taiwan's Chen Jing at the 1996 Summer Olympics, fan Chen Kun Chung unfurled a Taiwanese flag, in contravention of IOC rules (the Taiwan flag was prohibited at the Olympics under IOC regulations – the only national flag to face such restriction).

While police attempted to remove Chen and confiscate the flag, a second fan, Lee Chien Hsing, punched an officer in the mouth and pulled him down over some seats before both spectators were arrested.

Chen was charged with disorderly conduct and fined $100 after pleading no contest, while Lee was charged with one count each of simple battery and felony obstruction of an officer.

DAMAGING

In August 2008, according to reports in *The Guardian*, an Italian court awarded a Napoli fan – identified only as GDB €1,500. Why? Apparently, banners on display at the San Siro stadium in Milan which described Naples as the 'sewer of Italy' had caused him 'existential damage'!

Inter were liable for the payment.

IS THAT A RECORD?

In a promotion conceived by Chicago DJ Steve Dahl in July 1979, fans got admission to a doubleheader between the Chicago White Sox and Detroit Tigers for under a dollar, in exchange for bringing in a vinyl disco record to be blown up between games. The first game suffered a number of delays after fans threw their records, fireworks and beer cans onto the field, while the between-games explosion tore a large hole in the pitch, which was followed by thousands of fans invading the field, resulting in a near-riot. Some forty fans were arrested, and the second game of the doubleheader was forfeited to the Tigers.

WELL TRAINED

Russian authorities came up with a cunning way of cutting down the potential threat of fan violence when Dynamo Moscow and Dynamo Kiev were due to meet in July 1955.

A Kiev fan recalled:

As we got out of the subway train and stood on the platform, we heard a voice on the public address system announcing that the game would not take place. Thousands of spectators turned around and went back home. Imagine our surprise when we returned home, put on the radio and heard the beginning of the match that 'was not taking place'.

BEER BAN

Almost 1,000 Dutch fans had to watch their 2006 World Cup game against Ivory Coast in their underpants thanks to FIFA's rules about advertising from unauthorised sponsors. Dutch brewery Bavaria – one of the said unauthorised sponsors – had been giving away free orange lederhosen featuring their branding with purchases of their beer. When hundreds of fans arrived at the stadium decked out in their free lederhosen, officials insisted they would be denied entry, prompting the Dutch supporters to strip down to their underwear.

FIFA spokesman Tom Houseman described the giveaway as 'ambush' marketing – free publicity at the expense of official sponsors. He went on to say: 'The idea of hundreds of fans removing their trousers is always potentially amusing, and our suspicion is that trousers were chosen as an ambush tool specifically because of the publicity that fans taking them off would generate.' Bavaria said no sponsors had the right to tell fans what to wear.

LEG SLIP

A lady who attended a cricket match played at Kennington, London, in June 1737 between one side representing the Prince of Wales and another playing on behalf of Lord Sackville suffered an unfortunate accident during the match. 'The press was so great on the occasion that the poor woman, by the crowd bearing upon her, unfortunately had her leg broke,' reported the *London Evening Post*, adding that when the Prince heard of the incident 'he was pleased to order her ten guineas'.

RACING FOR EMANCIPATION

A racegoer was fatally injured when she dashed on to Epsom racecourse during the 1913 Derby and brought down the King's horse, Anmer, while it was in full flight. She died four days later from her injuries, by which time she had been named as suffragette Emily Davison, who was there protesting the cause of female emancipation.

In 2013 this most famous tale of spectator intervention was the subject of respected author Michael Tanner's *The Suffragette Derby*, while Ms Davison's motives were similarly scrutinised in that centenary year by numerous other writers and broadcasters – with 'national treasure' Clare Balding even getting in on the act – all dispensing myths, motives and interpretations in their efforts to explain Davison's actions.

FAN-TASTIC QUOTES

'They boo for a living in those places. We played on Christmas Eve and they even booed Santa Claus.'

– American football side Houston Oilers' coach from 1984 to 1989, Jerry Glanville, on Cleveland and Cincinnati fans.

'To be an intelligent fan is to participate in something. It is an activity, a form of appreciating that is good for the individual's soul, and hence for society.'

– American journalist George F. Will in the introduction to his 1990 book *Men at Work: The Craft of Baseball*.

'You know what they do when the game is rained out? They go to the airport and boo bad landings.'

– Bob Uecker, who played for the Philadelphia Phillies from 1966–67, on their fans.

'The fans who give me stick are the sort of people who still point at aeroplanes.'

– Arsenal footballer Ian Wright, 1997.

'Player loyalty is a supporter's fantasy, not a moral reality.'

– Simon Barnes of *The Times* on player response to fans, 11 February 2013.

'Maybe the fan was trying to tell me I stink.'

– Neal Morton, University of Michigan basketball player, after a deodorant was thrown towards him during one of their home matches.

'We do have the greatest fans in the world, but I've never seen a fan score a goal.'

– Scotland boss Jock Stein, 1982.

'To all the fans. U are not forced to buy season tickets … Or pay our wages … Please remember that…'

– Ill-advised tweet from Newcastle player Nile Ranger to supporters as Newcastle crashed to 1–2 home defeat to bottom three Reading in the 2012–13 season, slipping very close to the relegation places themselves.

FAN NEVER FLAGGED

Cleveland Indians baseball team fan, Charley Lupica, a local grocer, was so upset to find his team languishing in seventh place in their division in May 1949 that he 'held a vigil' on the platform of a flagpole sixty feet above his deli, declaring that he would not come down until the team were heading the table.

Lupica had been arguing with some local New York Yankee fans, telling them if they loved the Yankees so much they should move to New York, to which jibe they responded, 'If you love the Indians so much, why don't you sit on a flagpole until you die up there?' Which he very nearly did.

The Indians did move up to fourth but 117 days later had peaked in third, at which point Charley was finally talked down by club owner Bill Veeck, who sent a truck to transport Charley and the flagpole to the Municipal Stadium, where 34,000 Indians fans cheered as he finally came down.

While he was up there he had even missed the birth of his son!

SUICIDAL SHOWDOWN

A fan had provocative confrontations with North Melbourne coach Dean Laidley at both half-time and full-time of the May 2006 AFL match they lost to St Kilda at Telstra Dome.

The supporter twice made rude remarks, to which Laidley responded with an honest comment, 'we are all hurting', and an invitation into the club's locker rooms so the fan could see for himself how badly the Kangaroos players were feeling about their consistently poor on-field performance; the incident was shown live on Australian television.

The incident ended in tragedy when the fan, a man in his late thirties, committed suicide by throwing himself in the path of an oncoming train the next morning, but the man's family, the Victoria police and North Melbourne officials believed the death was unrelated to the incident at the game.

Laidley, who would later coach St Kilda, said he was 'shattered' over the event.

MAX-IMUM PUNISHMENT

The *Boston Globe* reported in May 1981:

Cedric Maxwell got the bad news yesterday. His run-in with a Philadelphia fan last Friday night during game six of the Eastern Conference finals at the Spectrum will cost him $2,500.

The National Basketball Association announced the fine yesterday against Maxwell, who charged into the stands and shoved a middle-aged man whose remarks he apparently took exception to … Maxwell was trying to get position under the Celtics backboard and was shoved out of bounds by Darryl Dawkins of the 76ers.

The momentum of Dawkins' shove carried Maxwell into the lap of a fan who was cheerleading in front of his front-row seat. Maxwell picked himself up and headed back to the court. Suddenly, he stopped and went back to charge the man, who was knocked over his chair. The fan was not identified.

Apparently, the fan 'stabbed' Maxwell with a pencil. Can't see the point, myself!

FANS HORSING ABOUT

The owners of the brand-new Wembley Stadium had boasted that 125,000 fans would be able to watch the 1923 FA Cup final between Bolton and West Ham. So it was unfortunate that well over 200,000 turned up, pouring into the ground, spilling onto the playing surface, and holding up kick-off for some forty-five minutes. There was, though, little, if any, reported trouble and the heroes of the hour were a police constable and his white horse, who kept the peace and inched the crowd back behind the touchlines so that the game could go ahead for Bolton to win 2–0.

GIVEN A COATING

Bottom-of-the-table Northern League side Elswick Rangers turned up for their game at Auckland Town in March 1890 with just four men – who were augmented by 'local volunteers', including, in goal, an Auckland fan who 'attired as an ordinary spectator, did not deign to remove his coat'. The patchwork side lost 10–2.

STAN THE FAN'S MAN

Aston Villa skipper Stiliyan 'Stan' Petrov was diagnosed with acute leukaemia in March 2012, aged thirty-two. The condition was diagnosed following tests after he developed a fever not long after Aston Villa's 3–0 defeat to Arsenal.

When Petrov, who wore a number 19 shirt, subsequently visited Villa Park for a game against Chelsea, the crowd gave him an ovation when the clock showed nineteen minutes. Fans continued regularly with this tribute in subsequent games.

On 2 August 2012, it was announced that Petrov's leukaemia was in remission, but fans continued the 'nineteen' tradition. However, at the start of the 2013–14 season, Petrov asked fans to discontinue the honour.

DEAD EMBARRASSING

Officials at HFS Loans League side Congleton staged a minute's silence in honour of a recently deceased fan at a February 1993 game against Rossendale. Arriving for the match and reading of the demise of the supporter in the programme, 83-year-old Fred Cope was appreciative of the gesture but pointed out that he was very much alive.

SNOW STORM

Booze was at the fore once again during day two of the final Ashes Test between Australia and England at the Sydney Cricket Ground in 1971: not only were beer bottles and cans thrown onto the outfield, but English quickie John Snow, who had bowled a bouncer at Terry Jenner, forcing the Aussie to retire from the field, found himself booed and manhandled by a drunk and drug-affected fan on the boundary.

England skipper Ray Illingworth took his team off in protest, but when the umpires warned that the Ashes would be awarded to Australia in their absence, England's boys returned to the field. Before they could begin, though, yet another beer can flung from the crowd hit a sight-screen attendant, who had to be carried unconscious from the field on a stretcher. Fourteen fans were arrested for offensive behaviour and a further 190 ejected.

DID THEY HAVE TO?

When the players of Didcot second team and Pennanians rugby union sides came to blows during a 1991 fixture, the beleaguered referee called for help from watching fans to help him break up the scrap; instead, they joined in.

FUNKY FANS

A US psychiatrist warned prior to the 2013 Super Bowl final between San Francisco 49ers and Baltimore Ravens that medical 'withdrawal' symptoms could be felt by fans across the country on Sunday night after the game, 'leaving thousands in an off-season funk due to a chemical imbalance in the brain left by the love of the game'.

Dr Angelos Halaris, medical director of Adult Psychiatry at the Loyola University Chicago Stritch School of Medicine, said some fans would need to watch reruns to ease themselves down.

He claimed fans' brains create dopamine on watching the crowning glory of their favourite sport. But when the big match finishes, no matter who wins or loses, they can 'feel bereft by the absence of this happiness neurotransmitter'.

And the comedown can be hard, leaving sufferers depressed and lonely. Take care of each other, sports fans.

'00 ARE YA?

Striding towards the green at the final hole of the 1981 Open Championship at Sandwich, Bill Rogers was stopped by a member of the local constabulary and made to prove that he wasn't a gatecrashing spectator. On the contrary, Rogers was about to win the Championship – which must have been some consolation to him.

PRINCELY STAND AGAINST RACIST FANS

Kevin-Prince Boateng of AC Milan, who walked off the pitch when racially abused by fans during a match against Pro Patria in January 2013, faced no disciplinary action – as you might expect.

His teammates followed him off and the friendly was abandoned. 'We cannot discipline a gesture of support for a man who has been victim of vulgar insults purely on the basis of the colour of his skin,' said an Italian FA official.

However, when, in July 2013, AC's Kevin Constant accused Sassuolo fans of racially abusing him and walked off, club officials criticised his actions and he was fined €3,000. Sassuolo, meanwhile, were fined €30,000.

TIE DOWN

Tie Domi had acquired a reputation as one of the NHL's most legendary enforcers, gaining more penalty minutes than any other player in the history of the Toronto Maple Leafs and reaching third overall in the entire history of the NHL.

So it was no great surprise that Domi lost his cool during a 2000–01 game in which a drunken Philadelphia Flyers fan began abusing him as he was sitting in the penalty box. Domi used his water bottle to spray a heckler, prompting another Flyers fan, Chris Trumbore, to begin yelling at him and climbing up the glass. The glass panel gave way, and the fan fell into the penalty box where Domi was seated, whereupon the player began throwing punches at his would-be assailant.

Flyers' management reportedly received a fine for not having better crowd control and security in place. Domi was fined $1,000, but received no suspension.

LAMPING LAMPS

Trainee architect Timothy Smith, 18, of Datchet, near Slough, was given a three-year football banning order and fined £300 plus £50 costs at Haringey Magistrates' Court in March 2007.

Chelsea had beaten Tottenham 2–1 recently, which proved too much to bear for Smith, who ran onto the pitch and attempted to punch the Chelsea and England midfielder Frank Lampard.

Leaving a host of stewards in his wake, Smith sprinted towards Lampard. But the distance the less-than-fit thug had to cover to reach his target took its toll, and the resulting punch was somewhat puny.

As Lampard sidestepped the would-be wallop, Smith fell to the floor, whereupon the entire Chelsea team set about him.

DOGGED BY MISFORTUNE

Paul Durkin evidently didn't relish being hit by a hot dog thrown from the crowd by a fan during an Oldham vs. Chelsea FA Cup tie in January 1999: the referee responded by asking for police protection.

LEG-ENDARY INJURY

On 1 January 2013, the *Daily Mail* reported that world tennis no. 1, Novak Djokovic, had suffered a 'bizarre injury scare' in a 'fans' crush'. Apparently he had been signing autographs at the Hopman Cup during his preparation for the Australian Open 'when he hurt his leg as fans pushed towards him'.

FANS SENTENCED TO DEATH

An Egyptian court sentenced twenty-one people to death in late January 2013 over football riots that had killed seventy-four people the previous year.

The verdict itself caused deadly violence.

The riots – Egypt's worst-ever football disaster – had begun after a top-league game at Port Said stadium on 1 February 2012.

Clashes broke out between rival fans of clubs Al-Masry and Al-Ahly. Fans invaded the pitch, hurling stones and fireworks at the visiting Cairo fans and attacking Ahly players as the match ended. Most victims died of concussion, cuts and suffocation.

The incident led to the suspension of the league.

The court ruling caused anger in Port Said, where

over thirty people died as supporters of the defendants clashed with police. All twenty-one defendants sentenced to death were Al-Masry fans. When the verdicts were announced by a judge in the Cairo court, relatives of victims cheered.

At time of writing it was unclear whether the verdicts would ultimately be enacted.

BALLBOYGATE!

The world of football went ever so slightly crazy on the night of 23 January 2013 when, with his side 2–0 down at Swansea in the semi-final of the Capital One Cup and facing elimination, Eden Hazard went to collect the ball from a 'self-declared massive Swansea fan' – as controversial defender Joey Barton later described him – who was a ballboy for the game.

The ballboy did not seem over-keen to give the ball to Hazard, and actually appeared to fall on it in an effort to hang on to it to allow more time to elapse. Hazard did not take this very well and endeavoured to get the ball, initially using his arms and hands and then appearing for all the world to kick the ballboy in the ribs.

Hazard ended up with a three-match ban and the ballboy, who, it transpired, was the seventeen-year-old

son of a wealthy Swansea director, and who had adver-
tised his intention of attempting to time-waste during
the game on the social network Twitter, was abused and
admired apparently in equal measure.

Media commentators, players and officials queued up
to give their opinion of the incident, which, if nothing
else, showed how the obvious tends to be ignored until
it is highlighted, at which point everyone is up in arms
about what they have always known – in this case, that
ballboys often take it on themselves to waste time, and
are quite probably even encouraged, albeit indirectly, by
clubs and managers.

Charlie Morgan, the ballboy, enjoyed an initial flush
of fame, until his father stepped in and imposed a media
blackout on him!

OH YES, I'M THE GREAT IMPOSTOR...

Many fans have managed to influence, enhance, affect
and even immortalise sporting events but very few
have actually managed to take part, or officiate, in them
uninvited.

Take a – sadly posthumous, having died in June 2011
– bow, Barry Bremen.

From 1979 to 1986, Bremen posed as a Major League

Baseball umpire in the World Series, a player in a Major League Baseball All-Star Game, a player in a National Basketball Association All-Star Game, a referee in the National Football League, a Dallas Cowboys cheerleader and a professional golfer.

Born and bred in Michigan, Bremen worked as an insurance and novelty goods salesman and as a marketing executive, but his leisure time was rather more colourfully spent.

A self-proclaimed 'jock', the 6ft 4in. Bremen regularly played touch football, basketball and softball, and his lanky athleticism paid off when he wangled his way into games across the sporting spectrum. His wife Margo believed he was 'fulfilling a grand fantasy to be in the limelight. He feels if you have no guts you have no glory in your life.'

Bremen first dipped his toe into the waters of sporting participation in December 1979, when he posed as a Dallas Cowboys cheerleader at a Cowboys–Redskins game held at Texas Stadium. In preparation, he lost 23lb, practised drag routines with his wife, had a replica Dallas Cowboys cheerleader uniform custom-made and shaved his legs.

On the big day, Bremen burst onto the scene in boots, hot pants, falsies and a blonde wig. He got out only one cheer – 'Go Dallas!' – before Cowboys security had him hogtied and handcuffed. You might think that would have been enough to deter Bremen, especially when the team hit him with a $5,000 lawsuit for trespassing and creating a nuisance, and endeavoured to have him banned from Cowboy games for life.

Not so. After a brief absence to gather his spirits, he returned to the sporting world on 4 February 1979, when he donned a Kansas City Kings uniform and joined the pre-game warm-ups for the NBA All-Star Game at the Pontiac Silverdome. He was 'outed' by Otis Birdsong, who really *was* a Kansas player, who asked, 'How come you're on my team and I don't know you?'

Later that year, he made a foray into the world of golf, appearing at the Inverness Club in Toledo, Ohio, where he sneaked in to play a practice round with Wayne Levi and Jerry Pate. Bremen, who boasted a handicap of seven, later noticed that Pate, the Open winner three years earlier, had dropped out of a threesome with Byrne and Levi after nine holes, so he joined the two on the back.

But he excelled himself when, at the 1980 US Open, he posed as bona-fide player Chuck Moran, took a courtesy car to the course, mingled with the other pros – including Jack Nicklaus – then joined players Jim Thorpe and Bobby Nichols at the fourth and played the rest of the round alongside them.

That year was a busy one for Bremen: he also turned

up at a World Series game where, clad as an umpire, he walked out to home plate with five real officials before he was rumbled. In 1981 he posed as a line judge referee at Super Bowl XV at the Louisiana Superdome in New Orleans.

Costumes were a particular passion, though the more outlandish ones sometimes impeded him – as in 1982 when he was denied access to the Pontiac Silverdome, the venue for Super Bowl XVI, thanks largely to him having arrived dressed as the San Diego Chicken.

At the 1985 US Open, Bremen played a practice round with Fred Couples, who later said, 'I had a great chuckle with him.' Bremen subsequently joined Couples during his round, as the pro related afterwards:

> He comes out of the shrubs on the second hole and hits this tee shot that buzzes the spectators ... He had this big wig on and a visor and looked a little out of place, but we didn't care. He just did his deal and had a great time. It didn't take long for people to scream out, 'Who is that guy?' I mean the cat was out of the bag after a couple holes, but we didn't get in trouble and no one came out to get him.

Bremen said that out of all his stunts, he was proudest of his golf antics. 'I was out there for the longest time,' he said proudly, 'and I was never caught.'

YABBA DABBA DOO

Perhaps the first fan in Australian sport to transcend the event and become an attraction in his own right was Stephen Harold Gascoigne (1878–1942), aka Yabba, who would hurl witty comments and occasional abuse at those cricketers and rugby league players unfortunate enough to attract his attention.

He was usually to be seen at The Hill in Sydney Cricket Ground, from where he would pour scorn on anyone he perceived to be under-achieving:

'I wish you were a statue and I were a pigeon.'

'Your length is lousy, but you bowl a good width.'

'Leave our flies alone, Jardine. They're the only friends you've got here.' (To English cricket captain Douglas Jardine, when Yabba spotted him swatting at flies.)

'Whoa there, he's bolted!' (As a becalmed batsman finally managed a run.)

'Send 'im down a piano, see if 'e can play that!'

'Those are the only balls you've touched all day!' (To an English batsman adjusting his box in between overs.)

'Put a penny in him, George, he's stopped registering.' (To an umpire who read gas meters and emptied cash boxes for a living, when a batsman at the crease was scoring slowly.)

Yabba became so well known that England's Jack

Hobbs, who was playing his final Test in 1929, acknowledged him, and he would often be interviewed by the media when play was slow or delayed.

Yabba can be seen to this day: on 7 December 2008 a bronze statue of him, sculpted by Cathy Weiszmann, was unveiled at the Sydney Cricket Ground in The Hill area of the new stand. It depicts Yabba in characteristic pose, one hand acting as a megaphone, in the act of delivering one of his famous interjections.

FAN-ANCIAL BLISS

The life of one Saracens rugby union club fan changed forever one Tuesday night in November 2009, as Stuart Tinner won £250,000 at Wembley Stadium.

The Sarries supporter from Welwyn in Hertfordshire won the Sarries Crossbar Challenge to kick a ball from 30 metres and hit the crossbar.

Stuart took to the hallowed Wembley turf at half-time to take the kick in front of nearly 47,000 fans, and his effort struck the middle of the crossbar to leave him a quarter of a million quid richer.

He said, 'I really can't believe it. It's an amazing feeling – I'm still in a daze. It won't change me; I'm still going to work in the morning, but what a night it has been.'

And on 25 January 2013, one lucky Miami Heat basketball team fan was also left in dreamland after sinking a $75,000 shot from the halfway line – which he celebrated by rolling around on the floor with LeBron James.

Michael Drysch, 50, over-armed his effort clean through the hoop during the break at the end of the third quarter of the Heat's 110–88 win over Detroit, and was immediately mobbed by the 6ft 8in. NBA superstar, who bear-hugged the computer technician to the floor.

James said, 'When he wound up I was like, "Oh no, there's no way." When it dropped, that was awesome. I would have probably air-balled that one in that situation.' Drysch became the first person ever to land the 'Half-Court Hero' contest, which is funded by one of James's sponsors, Carmex.

ROOTER RIOT

Back in 1916 the game of football, or soccer as it became better known there, was already making inroads in the USA, to the extent that there was a National Challenge Cup, which had launched in 1913, attracting teams from as far west as Chicago and as far north as Niagara Falls – and it stirred up passions, too.

The 1916 final saw a lively crowd of 10,000 flock to Pawtucket to see two of the big noises of the sport, Bethlehem FC, from 60 miles north of Philadelphia, and Fall River Rovers, from New England, who had made that stage from a starting line-up of over eighty clubs.

The *Pawtucket Evening Times* takes up the story with the game entering its final minute, with Bethlehem a goal up thanks to a controversial penalty:

The Rover rooters, distinguished by the yellow cards in their hats, kept up a fearful din of disapproval. Suddenly, just as Referee Whyte was about to blow his whistle and end the game, a short, thick-set man was seen running out toward the centre of the field.

That was all there was needed to precipitate a riot. In an instant the field was black with people, and Referee Whyte disappeared in a vortex of struggling humanity. The players formed a cordon about the official and, aided by the police, who used their clubs freely, Whyte was dragged to the J & P Coats clubhouse, his shirt torn from his back and his body black and blue from the pummelling he received.

LIFE'S A BEACH

L iverpool's spirits took a bit of a hammering when they were beaten by a goal in October 2009 – not unusual, perhaps, except that this one was scored when a beach ball thrown onto the pitch at Sunderland by a fan diverted the match ball into the net.

Liverpool's stuttering season took a turn for the worse as they went down 1–0 to the freak goal.

Sunderland, aka the Black Cats, grabbed all three points when a Darren Bent shot was allowed to stand after deflecting in off the beach ball, which a Reds fan had thrown onto the pitch.

Callum Campbell later told the *Sunday Mirror* he was afraid to leave his house after Liverpool's defeat at the Stadium of Light. The teenage fan responsible revealed his 'anguish' over the incident, which caused him to be physically sick and led to death threats.

'When I got home I went into the garden and threw up. I was physically sick – and that's before the death threats started appearing on the internet the next day,' Campbell said.

I watched it over and over again, and I still can't work out how it happened. But my mum tells me it wasn't my fault – and that's what I have to believe.

The referee should never have allowed the goal. I just hope the real fans understand and forgive me. But I accept I shouldn't have thrown it onto the pitch in the first place.

SNAKING ALL OVER

Fans at the Sydney Cricket Ground utilised a rain delay by creating the world's longest beer snake, reported the London paper *Metro*.

Bored by the two-hour hold-up during their one-dayer against Sri Lanka on 20 January 2013, fans on either side of the ground began building snakes by stacking plastic beer glasses together.

Both snakes grew to such an extent they met in the middle of the stadium.

The snake reached an estimated 175 metres [574 feet] in length when the scoreboard at the SCG announced that a new beer snake record had been set, producing huge cheers from the 22,000 crowd and beating the previous puny record of a mere 23 metres set by a crowd at the WACA ground in Perth in 2007.

The 'Beer Snake' phenomenon was first reported at a January 2001 game in Sydney and the Sydneyite effort has yet to be bested.

MAKING MINCEMEAT OF THEM

A record crowd, paying gate receipts of £48, attended the Lancashire League grudge match of the 1889 season, between Todmorden and Rochdale.

But the pro-Todmorden fans were a little subdued when their side collapsed to 59 all out.

Rochdale, beaten just once all season, seemed set for an easy victory.

Todmorden claimed an early wicket but appeals for a second, a stumping of noted batsman Briggs, were rebuffed by the umpire, which somewhat miffed the Todmorden faithful and 'instead of giving the umpire credit for an honourable decision, the spectators raised a storm of hooting and hissing'.

The Todmorden bowlers charged in and Rochdale struggled to 21 for 5.

Hoping to influence the outcome of the game, some Todmorden fans 'were at their worst. They induced a hot-pie vendor to stroll towards the wickets towards the Rochdale umpire and, as the other (nursery rhyme) pie man did to Simple Simon, "give him of his wares" in reward for the decision as to Briggs,' reported the *Rochdale Observer*.

When the pie man got near enough, however, Rochdale

batsman Handley (who went on to make 38) just glared at him and raised his bat as if to knock the whole basket of pies into mincemeat. The pie man thereupon repented of his generosity, and quickly took himself back to the ropes.

Extraordinarily, the game ended tied, but as a result of the fans' actions the Rochdale committee decided to cancel the next season's Todmorden fixtures.

BY GEORGE, HANG ON TO THE JOB

George Raynor was one of the first Englishmen to manage abroad: in 1948 he coached Sweden, and in the mid-1950s he became boss of Italian side Lazio – but it wasn't exactly plain sailing, as he explained in his auto-biography, *Football Ambassador at Large* (whose snappy title possibly explains why the book wasn't a bestseller!).

Raynor recalled the reaction to a controversial team selection: 'Our goalkeeper had been weak, so I substituted an old man of something like thirty-five years of age. The newspapers called me crazy and demanded that I resign.'

The fans went further, and a club director warned Raynor that 'the rabid supporters had set up some gallows, and that they would hang him if Lazio lost'.

Fortunately for George, Lazio won and he lived to tell the tale.

But Raynor remained wary of Lazio fans after that – his butcher was one, too, and Raynor said, 'If we lost, there would be no deliveries. And if we lost a couple of matches he would leave a small wooden coffin outside the door.'

ROLL MODEL FOR FANS?

Peter Norman of East Grinstead, West Sussex, wrote to *The Times* on 4 January 2010, recalling Harringay Arena's staging of roller skating speedway in the late 1940s:

Sir, Roller skating speedway, featuring men and women, was popular in the late Forties when for a couple of winter seasons it filled Harringay Arena to capacity.

Players punched, tripped and barged each other around the circuit. Few reached the finishing line, with most being thrust over the guard rails where fighting continued off track. Often the audience joined in. One buxom girl was dressed as a Native American with a feathered headdress. My father thought she was splendid. The council and the police thought otherwise, and the event was banned because it encouraged civilian unrest.

This forgotten sport did indeed cause fan frenzy in London, and journalist Tom Stenner was there to see it:

> So great was the excitement that the crowd got out of hand at times – women in particular worked themselves to a frenzy and I saw one, little more than a girl, with a baby in her arms, rush up to an American skater and give him a hefty swipe on the jaw.

The sport involved teams – men and women in separate crews – starting off in a pack, until one would break away and skate round the track at top speed in an attempt to circle the pack. One point was earned for passing one opponent, two points for passing two, up to a maximum of five for overtaking an entire team.

It sounded simple, but wasn't: they could be prevented from overtaking by virtually any means – blocking, pushing, tripping, fighting etc.

Stenner reported on a particular meet where a pig's head thrown at the ref put him out of action, while an armrest from a chair nearly broke a competitor's ankle, whereupon 'some of the skaters jumped the rails, climbed up the crowded terraces and went for their assailants. Blows were given and exchanged, players and spectators wrestled each other.'

Sounds ripe for a revival!

ICE SAY – BRIT FANS IN HOCKEY RIOT

In 1937 the destination of the Ice Hockey World Championship came down to a showdown between Canada and Great Britain – with the decisive game played at Harringay, where the home side were rated narrow favourites.

The match was to be officiated by neutral refs, but the first hint of problems emerged when it became obvious that neither of them was capable of keeping up with the pace of the game – 'and they adopted a compromise by standing by or sitting on the barrier whenever possible', wrote journalist Tom Stenner, who included a report of the match in his 1959 book, *Sport for the Million*.

When Canada took the lead through a clearly offside goal, the 9,000-strong crowd of mainly Brits began to chant 'we want a ref', and prolonged booing and catcalling broke out.

The game was held up until order could be restored, but when play resumed Canada 'scored' another offside goal – at which point, wrote Stenner, 'spectators literally saw red. They hurled everything they could lay hands on at the referees and even at the players. Silver and copper coins rattled like hail on the ice, rubber rings from the wooden seats and chair cushions were hurled from the crowded terraces.'

Then a Canadian supporter jumped onto the ice, threatening to take on 'any durned Britisher'.

> Scores jumped the barriers to take up the challenge. A hunting party made a dead set for the referees, who were chased into the corridors – as they ran, missiles were hurled at them and one tripped and fell, but was up in a flash just in time to escape his belabouring pursuers.

Then, with things getting out of hand, someone came up with an inspirational action:

> A gramophone record was put on and as the turntable revolved the strains of the national anthem were heard. In a moment the uproar became a mere noise, the noise a murmur.
>
> Those in the stands jumped to their feet, rioters in the corridors stood rigidly to attention and all joined in the singing as 'God Save The King' went winging and crashing into the glass roof above.

Amazingly, the game then resumed, with Canada eventually skating out 3–1 winners and a contingent of Canadian sailors who had attended the match being drafted in to ensure their countrymen were able to reach their dressing rooms in safety!

OF-FISH-IAL FAN PROTEST

Hungarian fans threw dead fish on the pitch during the football international against Australia in February 2000, presumably to the great dismay of all others in attendance. Their piscine tribute turned out to be a protest at a cyanide spill by a part-Aussie owned company which allegedly killed wildlife in two Danube tributaries.

ULTRA BAD TASTE

'Play Ultras', an Italian board game celebrating the exploits of rampaging hooligan fans, modelled on Monopoly and selling for €49, caused controversy when unveiled in November 2012. The game swapped Monopoly's car, hat and boot for miniature hooligans armed with belts, sticks and bars.

Players have to get past baton-wielding riot police figurines to reach a football stadium. The winner is the player who gets the largest number of his pieces into the stadium to watch the game – while avoiding a stay in hospital. Players also throw a dice to eliminate opposing fans by fighting them, stealing their banners and hospitalising them.

Giacomo Lonzi, one of the game's developers, defended Play Ultras and insisted he was not encouraging violence. 'I am an ex-Ultra against any form of violence,' he told *Corriere della Sera*. 'The message is: go wild on the board with the dice – but stay calm when you go to a match.' An English-language version was reportedly being prepared.

WOODS YOU BELIEVE IT?

Tiger Woods breathed a sigh of relief after narrowly making the cut at the Abu Dhabi Championship in January 2013.

Only he hadn't – because a couple of golf fans pointed out a two-stroke error which sent him packing.

Woods had taken a free drop after his ball had become embedded in sand, which is not permitted. The resultant penalty left him with a seventy-five on the day, putting him three over for the tournament – missing the cut by a single stroke.

Woods's drive on the fifth had landed in a bed of vines. Woods and his partner, Martin Kaymer, thought the ball was embedded in the vines, so he took the drop.

But 'an embedded ball relief is through the green but in ground other than sand', said European Tour chief referee Andy McFee, adding that after it occurred, the spectators were overheard questioning whether it was appropriate, and one duly alerted the European Tour to the infraction.

FEMALE FAN FRENZY

Violent female fans are a rarity these days, but it appears that this was not always the case – particularly at sporting contests in Australia, and specifically at Aussie Rules games.

As a provincial Melbourne paper, *The Argus*, observed in July 1896, 'The woman "barracker" has become one of the most objectionable of football surroundings. On some grounds they actually spit in the faces of players as they come to the dressing rooms, or wreak their spite much more maliciously with long hat pins.'

And the paper described what had happened in a recent home North Melbourne game against Collingwood, where

a 'lady' had the enviable honour of starting the distur-
bance. As the players were coming in at half-time she
waited near the gate and struck [umpire] Roberts in
the face. Afterwards, her shrill voice as she leaned over

the fence added a high treble to the torrent of abuse rained on the unfortunate umpire whenever he approached.

North Melbourne had been trailing, launched a come-back but were beaten narrowly.

As the final bell was sounded, disgruntled Melbourne fans targeted the umpire again and he

had to run the gauntlet of this ruffianism to reach the dressing room. The moment he stepped through the gate, scores rushed at him like wolves and a scene of inde-scribable tumult followed. Fists and sticks were going and one man with some implement wrapped in paper was making desperate efforts to fracture someone's skull.

Thanks only to a joint effort by players from both sides, the umpire somehow made it to safety but even then needed a police escort to depart the ground unscathed.

ELEVEN-MILLION-DOLLAR BRAWL

The repercussions led to nine players being suspended without pay for a total of 146 games, which resulted in $11 million in salary being lost by the players. Five players were charged with assault, and eventually sentenced to a year of probation and community service. Five fans also faced criminal charges and were banned from attending Pistons home games for life. The Pacers–Pistons brawl (colloquially known as the Malice in the Palace) happened in a National Basketball Association game between the Detroit Pistons and Indiana Pacers on 19 November 2004, at The Palace of Auburn Hills in Auburn Hills, Michigan.

With under a minute left on the clock in the game between the Pacers and the Pistons, a fight broke out between players on the court.

The 'routine' on-court fracas escalated to legendary proportions after Detroit fan John Green threw a cup of beer at the combustible Pacers player Ron Artest. The NBA All-Star launched himself into the crowd to attack Green, but ended up mistakenly hitting someone else.

Artest's teammate Stephen Jackson decided he would enter the mêlée in the crowd and before long a full-scale brawl erupted.

Subsequently nine players received suspensions, with Artest the hardest hit, with an eighty-six game suspension, and Jackson being banned for thirty games.

The beer-throwing John Green was banned from attending Pistons home games for life.

FATAL OVERREACTION

The actions of two Peruvian football fans who rushed onto the pitch in an Olympics qualifying match precipitated a national crisis in their country and led to the deaths of over 300 people. With only two minutes left to run in the game, played on 24 May 1964, the referee disallowed an apparent equaliser for Peru against Argentina, and the pair burst onto the field in anger.

The spectators were arrested but that just aggravated the crowd even more, and violence began to spread, causing the referee, Angel Eduardo Payos, to suspend play, claiming police protection was inadequate.

Now the fans invaded the pitch en masse. Police responded and tear gas was thrown, while fans began to set parts of the stadium on fire. Those attempting to leave the stadium found themselves trapped behind closed steel shutters, and some 318 people were killed in the stadium alone.

The fighting spilled onto the streets and in total 500 were injured in the violence. A national state of siege was declared and the country's constitution was suspended before order was finally restored.

STONES THROWN

Dwight Stones, a bronze-medal winner in 1972, was odds-on favourite to win gold at the 1976 Montreal Olympics in the high jump.

But he found himself for the high jump with fans after launching a verbal attack against the Games organisers for failing to complete the planned roof to the stadium in which they were competing.

When the event got under way the local fans had not forgotten reported remarks by him calling all French Canadians rude.

When Stones emerged for the qualifying competition he was booed by the crowd. Whenever his name was announced he was booed again. When he began his run-up to jump he was booed. Whether he succeeded or failed with a jump he was booed.

The next day Stones tried to win the crowd over with a T-shirt featuring the slogan 'I love French Canadians'.

Track officials soon made him take it off.

The damage had been done and when it started to rain – the very point he had been trying to make about the lack of cover in the stadium – Stones was done for, and in the circumstances did well to emerge with a second bronze medal.

REF TAKES STICK ... STONES ... WITH KNOBS ON

Weighing in at 265lb, the wrestler Con O'Kelly brought his brute strength to the rescue of English boxing referee T. H. Walker at the Paris Olympics of 1924 when Walker controversially disqualified an Italian named Giuseppe Oldani for persistent holding.

Oldani reacted hysterically, throwing himself to the canvas, sobbing and appealing to his fans in the crowd, who rose to the occasion by pelting the official with sticks, stones and even the knobs of their fashionable walking sticks.

For over an hour the fans protested, and Walker seemed to be in danger of his life until a contingent of British, American and South African boxers led by the hefty O'Kelly saved him.

OSCAR WINNER

An Olympic gold-medal winner in 1992, Oscar de la Hoya went on to become one of the most success-ful and popular US boxers of all time, winning world titles and then moving into promoting fights.

His popularity came in very handy on one occasion

when, during the early 1990s, in his home town of Los Angeles, he was robbed in the street one night by five gun-toting thieves, who stole his wallet, containing $150.

Philosophical de la Hoya never expected to see wallet or cash again.

Yet just two hours later the wallet turned up on the porch of his home – complete with cash.

The word on the street was that the 'punks' who had stolen it had not at first realised who their victim was until they opened the wallet and found out. Being fans of his they had promptly tried to make good their mistake.

ON THE FLORE

James Florey, a student from Bracknell, ran onto the racecourse at Ascot and straight into the path of filly Papago during the 1994 Ribblesdale Stakes at the Royal meeting.

The 21-year-old racegoer suffered multiple injuries after being trampled by the horse in what was the fifth race. Florey was believed to have been drinking heavily.

Spectators at the scene of the accident, near the one-furlong pole, said that a group of three young men had decided to run across the track from the cheap course enclosure to the more expensive grandstand after the field in the Ribblesdale Stakes had passed by. When they made their dash, Mr Florey found himself trapped under the hooves of Papago, the mount of Michael Kinane, one of two stragglers at the rear of the nine-runner field.

'He came out from under the rail right in front of me,' Kinane said. 'We were fifteen lengths behind the others and he was looking the other way. I think he thought the race was over. I went straight into him, and my horse turned over and landed on top of me.'

Florey was warned off all British racecourses for five years.

MAKING A MARK

Aston Villa keeper Mark Bosnich found himself in big trouble when he ill-advisedly Nazi-saluted at Spurs fans during a league match at White Hart Lane on 12 October 1996.

The Aussie keeper was subsequently fined £1,000.

FANS COLD SHOULDER THEIR OWN TEAM!

Who would have believed that fans turning their back en masse on their team would become a popular feature of terrace life?

When in 1961 the extraordinary event began to occur after teams had scored, initially across Eastern Europe, it became particularly associated with supporters of Polish side Lech Poznan, although the move was originally known as the 'Grecque'.

The Polish fans brought the celebration with them when they played Manchester City during an October 2010 UEFA Europa League game – and the City supporters were so impressed that they adopted the ritual themselves, adopting the 'Poznan' name by which it is now universally described.

Occasionally, the celebration in which fans stand with their back to the pitch, link shoulders and jump on the spot in unison, has been used against City, notably by Leicester fans during an FA Cup game, and by Arsenal and Manchester United supporters.

The move reached as far as Australia, where in October 2012 fans of West Sydney Wanderers introduced it in their first ever game as a club, against the Central Coast Mariners at Parramatta Stadium.

NOT MUCH COP

'The Metropolitan Police have confirmed that they helped Arsenal stewards remove a banner from

Manchester City fans protesting at high ticket prices during the game at the Emirates on Sunday [13 January 2013]' reported the *Daily Telegraph*'s Paul Kelso.

The police claimed 'they only intervened to prevent a potential breach of the peace' and Arsenal claimed they acted because of the size of the banner, which had 'impeded the view of spectators, rather than because of what was written on it'.

If you say so.

JUST THE TICKET?

Six Newcastle United fans lost their legal fight against the club's plans to move them from their places to make way for more corporate hospitality seats in March 2000.

The six fans believed £500 bonds they bought in 1994 as season ticket holders entitled them to the same seat for ten years.

But Mr Justice Blackburne ruled after a four-day hearing that small print in the bond contract meant the club could move the fans.

Newcastle wanted to build a hospitality unit as part of a £45 million redevelopment of the ground, to accommodate an extra 15,000 supporters, taking the capacity to 51,000.

The fans, who brought the case on behalf of 2,000 other bond holders affected by the club's plans, claimed the club had no right to move them and was in breach of a promise made to them when the bonds were sold.

Jonathan Crystal, representing the fans, said: 'A guaranteed seat was a constant theme in interviews and publicity. The application form asked you to identify your particular seat. Anybody who filled in that form would have concluded that they were bonding that particular seat.'

Bonds were taken up by just over 7,000 fans, generating £3.6 million for the club.

The seats concerned were in the middle sections of two stands, and considered to have some of the best views in St James' Park.

The fans appealed the decision, but lost again.

The Lord Chief Justice, Lord Waller, ruled at the Court of Appeal that the club could legally move the fans, 'however sympathetic one may feel' towards them.

HIGHLY THOUGHT OF

Playing against the West Indies in 1973 at Sabina Park, Jamaica, Australia's Ian Chappell was fascinated to see a home fan in an unusual vantage point: 'As I looked up at one of the pylons there, about 200 feet up, was a man standing on a metal ledge about three or four inches wide, clinging on for dear life with one hand and clutching the ever-present bottle of West Indian rum with the other.'

Chappell kept his eye on the man as he took regular swigs from the bottle. After several hours 'he finished the bottle – but to my surprise he kept hanging on to it'.

Chappell asked one of the West Indies batsmen why he didn't just throw the bottle away, and was told, 'Keep watching.'

He did so, 'and soon enough I had my answer. I think I can say on behalf of the couple of hundred people below him on the pylon that they were eternally grateful he kept the bottle for the reason he did'!

SPUD FAN MASHED

During a 1997 Sahara Cup match against India in Toronto, Inzamam-ul-Haq stormed into the stands brandishing his bat, where he assaulted a member of the crowd, Shiv Kumar Thind, a Canadian-based Indian, who had reportedly been insulting Inzy and comparing him to 'several kinds of potato' on a megaphone.

According to one eyewitness, 'If not for the spectators

and security staff curbing him, he would have broken the head of that guy.' The man with the megaphone was no match for Inzamam and got mauled. Even when Canadian police took Inzamam back onto the field, he was trying to get back to the stands.

The *Toronto Star* reported:

For getting called several kinds of potato, Inzamam went into the stands and attempted to attack a mouthy fan, triggering a nasty mini-riot that could easily have escalated to world-wide ugly. Worse, a cricket bat appeared – no one is sure from where, although two witnesses said they thought they saw Inzamam call to the bench for one, and there was Inzamam apparently swinging his bat at the customer(s) before someone restrained him. He didn't appear to hit anyone with the bat. That is consistent; the Pakistani batsmen were off the mark all day.

LOSING STREAK

Streaker Robert Ogilvie clearly hadn't done his homework before deciding to gatecrash a 2008 one-day international between Australia and India.

He charged onto the playing surface and then made a crucial mistake: he headed for one of the Aussies at the crease batting. Big mistake. It was Andrew Symonds, never a man to shirk a challenge, who promptly shoulder-charged 26-year-old Ogilvie, leaving him in a crumpled heap on the floor.

Worse was to come for Ogilvie when he was later fined £700 for his troubles – while Symonds went unpunished. In fact, Cricket Australia commented: 'Symonds was dealing with self-preservation, which we support 100 per cent.'

Nor was he the first Aussie to take a hard line on streaking: in 1976, Greg Chappell was so angered when approached by a nude man at Auckland's Eden Park that he smacked him on the rear end with his bat.

ALDERMAN'S COLD SHOULDER

England had just reached a score of 400 in their first innings of the 1982 Ashes Test at the WACA ground in Perth, Western Australia, when between twelve and twenty fans invaded the pitch to celebrate.

Terry Alderman, who had just been hit for four, was then hit – 'thumped' as he would later call it – on the back of the head as one of the fans, nineteen-year-old Gary Donnison, originally from Yorkshire, passed him.

'I could see there were no police in the vicinity so I

decided to apprehend him,' said Alderman, who chased some 20 metres to crash-tackle Donnison but soon realised it had been a bad decision when he landed heavily on his right shoulder.

It was dislocated and he was stretchered off. He wouldn't bowl competitively again for another year.

Aussie journalist Scott Walsh later claimed: 'This time the Poms enlisted their fans to do their dirty work.'

Even Donnison's family disowned him after the incident, which saw him landed with a probation period and a $500 fine.

It was recently reported that Donnison had become a born-again Christian.

TALKING OF APPLES

Felix Carvajal, a postman from Cuba, was as keen to practise his English as he was to win the Olympic marathon he had entered in St Louis, USA, in 1904.

And the urge to speak the language may have cost the penniless unknown, who had lost his savings in a craps game en route to America, the chance of a medal.

Hitch-hiking to the venue, he turned up on the starting line wearing street shoes, long trousers, a long-sleeved shirt and a beret. The temperature would approach 90°F that day.

Another Olympian, a discus thrower, helped out by cutting the trousers off at the knees to make shorts after a fashion.

When the race started, Carvajal ran in a relaxed style, stopping regularly to chat to fans along the way, trying out his language skills and discussing race tactics.

However, with the heat increasing, he also 'borrowed' a couple of apples from a local orchard.

Later, a combination of the effect of the apples on his stomach and the lost time from fan engagement began to take their toll on his chances – but he still managed to finish a gallant fourth, close enough to the first three home for a medal to have been his had there not been the delays – avoidable and unavoidable – along the way.

BARRIER TO BECKS

Swirling with speculation, the football world was divided about AC Milan's 'timeshare' option on David Beckham at the beginning of the 2009 season – especially when the deal was extended until mid-July. Fans at his home team of LA Galaxy, however, were in little doubt about their feelings. During the first half of

Beckham's first game back at the Home Depot Center in July 2009, they directed a volley of abuse at the star, apparently prompted by his reported desire to remain with the Italian club.

At half-time, Beckham was restrained by security from trying to climb over a barrier to confront a drunk fan who, not content with verbal taunts, had run onto the pitch. The invading fan was arrested and banned from attending LA Galaxy home games for life, while Beckham was fined $1,000 for the incident. The fan's life ban was later lifted on appeal.

WOULD YOU BEER-LIEVE IT?

It became known as 'ten cent beer night'. For a 1974 game between the Cleveland Indians and the Texas Rangers at the former's home stadium, fans were served as many 10-ounce cups of beer as they wanted for just 10¢ each.

Predictably enough, there were numerous instances of drunken fans causing chaos, some throwing things, some running onto the field and some streaking.

The situation boiled over in the ninth inning when a sozzled supporter ran onto the field and snatched Rangers outfielder Jeff Burroughs's cap and glove. Burroughs's teammates promptly rallied to his aid, some wielding bats, along with manager Billy Martin – at which point hundreds of fans poured onto the field.

Indians boss Ken Aspromonte ordered his players to grab bats to protect their fellow players from the fans – and with good reason. In the resulting confusion, several players and officials were injured, including Cleveland pitcher Tom Hilgendorf, who was hit on the back of the head with a metal chair, and chief umpire Nestor Chylak, who was also hit on the head with a chair – this one thrown from the stands. As a result of the scuffle, nine people were arrested, and the game was forfeited to Texas. Cheers. Lesson learned?

Not really. In 1978, hockey tried its hand at a 'ten cent beer night' promotion at a game between the Fort Worth Texans and Dallas Black Hawks at the Will Rogers Coliseum. The game quickly descended into chaos, with brawls breaking out between fans in all corners of the stands. Five fans were injured and ten arrested.

As a result of this incident, significant discount alcohol promotions were finally – and sensibly – banned.

HE HAD A COBB ON

Detroit Tigers outfielder Ty Cobb showed the strength of team solidarity – though perhaps not in the best of circumstances – after his outburst during a baseball game against the New York Highlanders at Hilltop Park in New York in 1912. In the sixth inning, Cobb ran into the stands and assaulted a handicapped fan, Claude Lueker, after Lueker had heckled him throughout the first three innings.

You might expect the truculent Tiger to have been penalised for his actions, and indeed he was: Cobb found himself ejected, suspended indefinitely and fined $50. But Cobb's teammates obviously disagreed with the penalties, because, though not over-fond of Cobb himself, they all went on strike to protest against the suspension.

The stand-off ended after a heated ten days when the club threatened the striking players with indefinite suspensions. Cobb paid his fine and urged his teammates to return to the field in exchange for his suspension being lifted, which it duly was.

FAN-TASTIC QUOTES

'London witnessed an incursion of Northern barbarians – hot blooded Lancastrians, sharp of tongue, rough and ready, of uncouth garb and speech. A tribe of Soudanese [*sic*] Arabs let loose in the stand would not excite more amusement and curiosity.'

> – Observations of London's *Pall Mall Gazette* on the fans of 1884 FA Cup finalists, Blackburn Rovers.

'If I was a Hoops fan I'd be appalled at that sense of misplaced loyalty. It's QPR who pay your wages, son.'

> – Former Millwall striker Tony Cascarino showing his contempt for the recent penchant for players scoring against their former clubs not to celebrate afterwards. Shaun Wright-Phillips, who hadn't netted for over fifty games, finally did so to give QPR a memorable away Premier League win at Chelsea on 2 January 2013, but decided not to look remotely happy that he had done so, having once plied his trade for the opponents. I'm with Cas on that one!

'English people go to matches as a form of psychoanaly-sis – they turn up, have a good shout and then go home. That goes for everybody, bankers in Rolls-Royces and ordinary working people, too.'

– Arsenal player Emmanuel Petit in 1999.

'I'm this side of the line, you're that, and never the twain shall meet. If they do, I'll break your f***ing teeth.'

– Aussie wicket-keeper Rodney Marsh to a spectator who, in 1981, fielded a ball inside the boundary rope.

'Nobody ever bought a ticket to look at the audience.'

– Patrick Collins, *Mail on Sunday*, 2 December 2012.

'The stadium wasn't full but the right people were there – the British fans.'

– When Denise Lewis celebrated gold at the Sydney Olympics in 2000 it did not happen until late at night, by which time the stadium had somewhat emptied out.

'Surely no sport – other than soccer – would tolerate so many fatalities amongst its spectators. These are unnatural disasters, not acts of God; they are eminently preventable.'

– Respected US writer for *Sports Illustrated* magazine Steve Rushin, asking a rhetorical but pertinent question in the May 2001 edition of that publication.

'People [fans] object to being beaten by volunteers rather than the police. We told the volunteers that if they wanted to beat somebody they should take them outside and do it.'

– G. Y. Lele, Joint Secretary of the Indian Cricket Board of Control, on the behaviour of fans at matches, in 1993.

'One of the chief duties of the fan is to engage in arguments with the man behind him.'

– American humorist Robert Benchley.

GERMAN JOKER

The home crowd cheered as a German athlete led the men's marathon into the stadium for the final stages of the Munich Olympics in 1972.

But officials soon realised that Norbert Sudhaus, though first across the line, had been running without a number and was not a proper competitor – in fact he had put on his track gear while hiding among the crowds outside the stadium, and then joined the race, running only the last kilometre.

American Frank Shorter, who was actually born in Munich, was the real winner – the first person from the States to win the Olympic marathon in sixty-four years.

Assuming Sudhaus was the winner, the crowd began cheering the 22-year-old student before officials real-ised the hoax and security escorted him off the track. Erich Segal's cry to ABC television's US viewers of 'It's a fraud, Frank!' became known in the US as one of sports' most famous moments of commentary. Athletics fan Sudhaus's motivation for pulling the stunt was never made clear.

GOLDILOCKS'S UNLUCKY 13

Before a pitch invader dressed as Goldilocks decided to charge onto the pitch during a rugby union match between Bath and Sale on the evening of Friday 13 April 2012, it might have been a bright move to consider the date.

Goldilocks ran into more trouble than the three bears may have offered, by heading for fly-half Olly Barkley, who was not in a very good mood despite scoring all Bath's points, as they were on the way to losing the game 16–9. Barkley promptly tackled the intruder as fiercely as if she was a player for the opposition.

England international Barkley later tweeted:

'Judging by the reaction 2 tackling a drunk girl on Friday night, I may have to consider having it on my epitaph. My Grandad would be so proud.'

However, this Goldilocks was not a girl at all. In fact (s)he was a member of a stag party and (s)he had figured it would be safe to run towards Barkley, having met him before. Recalled Barkley:

Darren, our analyst, was on a stag do and I knew they were coming to the game. When the guy came on the field I thought I recognised him. The pitch invader was the 'stag', wearing a dress and a blonde wig.

He actually ran up and said, 'All right, Barks?'

Later, Barkley made amends by making a video for the stag's wedding, apologising for clattering him.

FANS START PLAY

Weather conditions were poor, but by 2 p.m. the sun was out – though there was no apparent thought being given to allowing the Edgbaston crowd in and getting the game under way.

Until, as ground administrator Robert Ryder later recalled of that 1902 England–Australia match, 'a great crowd assembled outside the ground. What I hadn't thought of was that two umpires and two captains would sit and wait for so long without making a decision.'

Then it happened – the decision was taken for them:

'The crowd broke in, and to save our skins we started to play at 5:20 on a swamp.'

FANS STOP PLAY

Lancashire's Archie MacLaren, who was also England skipper, was in no mood to continue play in his county's away match against Middlesex at Lord's in 1907, and explained why in a statement: 'Owing to the pitch being deliberately torn up by the public, I, as captain of the Lancashire XI, cannot see my way to continue the game, the groundsman bearing me out that the wicket could not again be put right.'

WHO NOSE WHY FAN WAS BANNED?

The *Edinburgh Evening News* reported in January 2013 that Hearts fan Francesco Fortucci, who had 'nose-dived' down the stands at Tynecastle during a recent match against local rivals Hibs, had become an internet sensation after his fall was shown on YouTube, where it had collected some half a million views in three days. Unfortunately for Fortucci, he was also banned from every football stadium in the UK as a result.

WHAT A FID-DLE!

The local race fans had decided that they would ensure the outcome of the big betting race – but they were outwitted by a quick-thinking jockey.

When Irish jump racing was in its infancy, a race was organised over open fields at Limerick in February 1833.

The locals decided they would resort to any tactics,

including stone throwing or pulling the rider from his mount, to prevent the only English rider, George Smith, coming out on top.

Warned of what might happen, Smith set off on his horse, Fidler, wearing his jockey kit and colours but, once under way, stopped to don an overcoat and hat before spurring his horse into a clear lead.

As he approached the fences guarded by stone-carrying spectators, Smith shouted at them to move clear as the favourite, who was winning, was just approaching.

Assuming Smith to be an interested party out following the course of the race, they did just that, permitting him to avoid personal damage and to romp to victory.

HEW WAS THAT?

As the runners turned for home during the 1913 Ascot Gold Cup, the previous year's St Leger winner, Tracery, was going well, four or five lengths clear, when, as an eyewitness account recorded,

emulating the example set by the militant suffragette whose rash interference with the runners in the Derby had thrown the field into confusion and led to her own death, some demented fanatic rushed out from the trees brandishing a revolver in one hand and a flag in the other.

Whalley, the rider of Tracery, tried to avoid the lunatic, but failing to do so, he and Tracery were brought down.

The previous year's winner, Prince Palatine, had to jump over Tracery, after which he swerved across the course, stood stock still, then started again – and won the race.

The 'lunatic', a man called Hewitt, whose revolver was indeed loaded, was severely injured.

REAL FAN RESPECT

All of the Real Sociedad side wore the name 'A Zabaleta' on their shirts in a 1998–99 Primera Liga game against Real Madrid – a mark of respect to the fan of that name stabbed to death by hooligans before a Cup match between the teams.

NAKED TRUTH

So many fans wanted to attend the naked sledging competition held annually at the German town of Braunlage that in 2013 it had to be scrapped because of health and safety concerns over the 25,000-plus people expected to arrive in the town for the event.

'When we get visitor numbers which are five times more than the inhabitants of the location, we've simply reached our logistical limits,' said Mike Brohl of the local radio station, 89.0RTL.

The event involved some thirty participants stripping off before sledging down the mountainside.

The organisers hoped to restage the contest in the future.

BARRED FOR LIFE

Toulouse rugby union star Trevor Brennan was warming up on the touchline during a 2007 Heineken Cup game against Ulster. Following a verbal altercation with spectators, Brennan jumped into the stands and punched Ulster fan Patrick Bamford.

Brennan alleged afterwards that the fan had abused his mother, but an enquiry into the incident ruled that no such abuse had ever taken place.

Rather, it was found that Brennan had taken umbrage because Ulster fans ridiculed the standards of his bar in Toulouse.

Brennan was handed a life ban from the sport. Presumably he spent some of his unexpected free time improving the standards of his pub.

THAT SHOED HIM!

Terry O'Reilly was the enforcer for the Boston Bruins ice hockey team. Nicknamed 'Bloody O'Reilly', he was infamous for the enthusiastic manner in which he would protect his teammates when things threatened to get a little hot on the ice.

So it must have been a brave or, more likely, foolhardy fan of the New York Rangers who, in a 1979 match, decided to steal the stick of the Bruins' Stan Jonathan and hit him with it.

Within seconds of the incident O'Reilly was climbing into the crowd, with the rest of the Bruins players following.

While O'Reilly grappled with the fan with the stick, another Rangers fan threw a shoe at him. O'Reilly's teammates began searching for a fan with just one shoe and upon finding him, beat him with his own footwear.

O'Reilly received an eight-game ban for his part in the fracas.

FRUITFUL PROTEST

Sri Lanka were awarded a victory by the match referee after Indian fans rioted during their 1996 Cricket World Cup semi-final.

The match was played at Eden Gardens, Kolkata, in front of a crowd unofficially estimated at 110,000. Chasing 252 to win, India slumped to 120 for 8 in the thirty-fifth over when sections of the crowd began to throw fruit and plastic bottles onto the field.

The players left the field for twenty minutes in an attempt to quieten the crowd. When they returned, more bottles were thrown onto the field and fires were lit in the stands.

Match referee Clive Lloyd awarded the match to Sri Lanka, the first default ever in a Test or One-Day International.

IT PAYS TO HOPE

Perhaps the first authenticated occasion on which genuine fans were *paid* to watch their team was in 1935, when the makers of the film *Hope of His Side* shelled out to supporters of Featherstone Rovers rugby league side, who were filmed watching a game against Broughton Rangers.

MAKING A SPECTACLE OF HIMSELF

It was reported in early 2000 that Ayr United fan Jason Stuart was fined £100 for throwing his spectacles onto the pitch after Celtic scored against his side in a recent game, despite his claim that 'my glasses just flew out of my hand'.

STAND-UP ROW

Fan heckling reached a new low during a timeout in a February 1995 NBA game between Portland Trail Blazers and the Houston Rockets, when Steve George allegedly taunted Rockets guard Vernon Maxwell about his wife's recent miscarriage. Maxwell responded by running a dozen rows into the stands and punching George in the face. George suffered a broken jaw, while Maxwell was ejected, suspended for ten games and fined $20,000.

CARTHAGE CHARIOT CIRCUIT CURSED?

According to respected archaeologist Anne Haeckl, who dug the ruins of a Roman circus at Carthage, the evidence suggests that fans attending chariot races at the site 'inscribed curses' against riders they wanted to lose, on lead tablets which were nailed up near the starting gate.

CHEERS

During the 1990 season, University of Michigan's American football side banned spectators from bringing marshmallows to matches, after fans took to throwing them at cheerleaders.

Whatever turns you on, I suppose.

On the other side of the pond, Bradford FC announced plans in November 2001 to frisk fans to prevent them from bringing confetti into the ground, as it was blocking drains. It wasn't explained why they were bringing in confetti in the first place.

I'LL BE DOGGONE – OR NOT

Jan Van Kook, 33, bought two season tickets to watch matches at Feyenoord in the 1999–2000 season – one for him, and one for his dog, Bo.

HANGING AROUND

Yugoslav boxing referee Miodrag Bozjak was dragged away by an irate crowd of fans after giving a decision against the local fighter in a 1991 bout in Titograd. Police reached the scene just in time to rescue the hapless official, who already had a noose tied around his neck.

WHAT THE FOX IS GOING ON?

Greyhound racing fan Colin Eastick caused chaos as favourite Swift Fox challenged rival Where's The Limo in the final stages of Sunderland's Mailcom Northern Puppy Derby in November 1990.

The 1,200 fans in attendance were enthralled as the two dogs battled it out with just 30 metres to run – only for Eastick suddenly to hurl a teddy bear onto the track.

It hit Swift Fox, just as the runner had looked like grabbing the lead.

Instead, 'panda'-monium broke out as racegoers chased after the culprit, who was trying to escape through the main gate of the stadium to a waiting car. He was finally caught by two plain-clothes policemen. A police spokesman later declared, 'If we hadn't taken him away the crowd might have lynched him.'

Eastick reportedly claimed, 'I did it because I think it is cruel to the dogs,' but many racegoers believed there may have been a far more sinister motive to do with betting on a dog which looked unlikely to win. He was later fined £100 by Sunderland magistrates, with £82 costs, a sentence which caused John McCririck to rage: 'Such oddly incomprehensible leniency will only encourage a rash of similar "jests"!'

SHOCKING

On 19 April 1995, Chelsea announced shocking news for their fans – they planned to erect an electrified fence to deter any of them from getting onto the pitch. The Greater London Council promptly announced it would take out an injunction to prevent them from so doing unless Chelsea promised never to turn the fence on. The plan was dropped.

RINGING THE CHANGES

American boxer Al Roberts was dominating the early stages of his 1920 fight against up-and-coming light heavyweight prospect Gene Tunney. Roberts detonated a big right hand to the jaw of Tunney, which buckled his knees, then moved in to finish him off, as someone in the crowd rang a bell, which Roberts took to mean the round was at an end, so he turned round to go to his corner – where his seconds had to convince him that the round was not yet over.

The delay gave Tunney the opportunity to unscramble his senses and regain his composure. From that instant on, the balance of the fight swung towards Tunney, who boxed beautifully and ended the fight in the seventh round.

Roberts disappeared into obscurity. Tunney went on to win the world heavyweight title. The bell-ringing fan remained anonymous.

NUTTY KIDDED OUT OF IT

Irish heavyweight 'Nutty' Curran was looking to improve his record by defeating experienced veteran 'Kid' McCoy, who had been around the block several times at this point, as he approached his fortieth birthday.

The two met in Paris shortly before the start of the First World War, and Curran was on top as he put McCoy down in round twelve.

The American was canny enough to stay down while he recovered his composure, and as he rolled over to get up, he spotted a glass which had been placed on the edge of the ring by a careless – or kindly – spectator.

McCoy grabbed the glass, which, it transpired, contained brandy. He downed it in one and received a boost to his system which saw him bounce back to score a points victory.

ROVERS AND OUT

Teenager David Stephenson Ingham Brennan Newton Noble Waldron Thompson Flynn Rodaway Hankin Collins James Welch plucked up courage to tell his Burnley-loving family, including mother Gillian, who named him after their 1974–75 team, that he was actually a Blackburn fan. 'They took it badly,' he said plaintively.

AIR WE GO

The final stages of the 2011 Cheltenham Festival race meeting's Ryanair Chase, won by Alberta's Run, was almost the scene of tragedy as a racegoer clad in a bright orange jacket and brandishing a placard complaining about the sponsoring airline came close to bringing down runners.

That cut little ice with jockey A. P. McCoy: 'If he'd brought me down I would have knocked him out.'

NOT A LEG TO STAND ON

When a horse bolted on the way to the start at Brighton races in 1877, the animal knocked down a spectator, whose leg was broken as a result.

The man subsequently wrote to the horse's owner, George Chetwynd, demanding damages and threatening to go to court if he didn't get them.

Chetwynd offered him a 25-guinea settlement, which was turned down.

The case duly came to court, where it transpired that the victim was a racecourse tout who described himself as a 'horse watcher' – which, given the circumstances, caused some hilarity in the court.

Chetwynd won the case, but had to pay his own, and the plaintiff's, costs.

WHAT AN APPALLING TOSSER

The *Racing Post* couldn't have put it any more starkly when they described why the police were called to Market Rasen's Ladies Night fixture on Saturday 14 August 2010 following the antics of drunken male racegoers:

'One of the party began to masturbate in front of the Tattersalls stand during a race,' reported Paul Eacott.

It was also reported that one of the group, who had been wearing fancy dress, ran onto the track.

'We are appalled by this incident,' commented Market Rasen managing director, Pip Kirby.

Former jump jockey Bryan Leyman, who was present, left before the last race, feeling 'sick in the stomach'.

There was a postscript when the *Racing Post* 'Chatroom' carried a note from the almost certainly pseudonymous 'Begonia Perrywinkle (Miss)', commenting:

'Had I been at Market Rasen that damned fellow would not have been left with the wherewithal to perform such a disgusting act again!'

GREAT DAY OUT

Oh, to have been at the Great Western Race Club in Victoria, Australia, in 1860 for the meeting attended by the *Ararat Advertiser*, whose reporter recorded: 'Supporters of the favourite, Black Boy, had surged onto the track to prevent the second horse, Punch, from winning. This caused supporters of Punch to set up a great barney around the judge, and it was as much as the one sober policeman could do to stop the fighting.'

About five o'clock, bystanders helped clear the course for the next race.

'Just as the last race was about to start, fighting broke out again and the day's racing terminated in a general free fight.'

ICY ATMOSPHERE

Salisbury racecourse rarely attracts headlines, but in the summer of 2009 it scored quite the most extraordinary public relations own goal when threatening to eject from the members' lawn a racegoer who had already spent £200 in the restaurant with his 75-year-old mother because the pair were spotted ... eating ice cream!

'We can't have people wandering around eating food. People pay extra for exclusivity in members. They don't expect to bump into someone carrying an ice cream,' declared general manager Jeremy Martin, from his office somewhere on Planet Zog.

There were protests, and, in a desperate effort to regain the PR initiative, at their next meeting Salisbury offered their first ninety-nine racegoers ... free ice cream, with one Mr Jeremy Martin declaring, 'We are a listening racecourse and will be allowing ice creams in members from now on. We won't be coning off special areas.'

WHAT THE BLAZES!

In February 1927, during Oakleigh Plate Day at Australia's Caulfield racecourse, the grandstand in the Guineas reserve section went up in flames after a lighted cigarette was carelessly discarded by a racegoer.

But they bred racegoers tough in those days, and a

contemporary report pointed out that the 'hundreds of people congregated on the two decks of the stand remained there until the race was over'.

Despite the stand continuing to burn all afternoon, only four people were injured, and the race meeting was duly concluded. It was later rebuilt at a cost of £60,000.

LEE-DER OF THE PACK

Pimlico racecourse in Baltimore, USA, stages a leg of the American Triple Crown of top races, the Preakness Stakes. In the 1999 meeting, drunken 22-year-old Lee Chang Ferrell scaled an infield fence, stood in front of eight charging horses during the Maryland Breeders Cup Handicap, and threw a punch at the favourite, Artax.

Ferrell told police he was trying to commit suicide when he slipped by security and got onto the track. He assumed a boxing stance and swung as horses thundered by him, missing Artax but striking jockey Jorge Chavez, who had to veer out of the way, hitting another horse.

Artax lost all chance of winning, and Pimlico had to refund the $1.4 million wagered on him.

Ferrell was sent for psychiatric testing, and later declared he was 'committed to sobriety'.

Artax suffered few ill effects, going on to win the Breeder's Cup Sprint and earn $1.6 million.

Three years later at the Preakness, Baltimore police officers removed their badges and nameplates and were caught on film hitting a spectator with a baton during a mêlée in the raucous infield, embarrassing the department when the video was aired nationally on television.

ROO MUST BE JOKING

Few racecourses can boast as mystical and atmospheric a backdrop as the volcanic Mount Diogenes, also known as Hanging Rock, immortalised in the haunting 1967 book by Joan Lindsay, and the 1975 movie *Picnic at Hanging Rock*.

The 500 racing fans who turned up for the Australia Day meeting at the tiny course in January 2011 were anticipating a great day's sport – which is what they got, even though they ended up seeing no horse racing at all.

But they did get to watch the fruitless efforts of course officials to keep the course clear of kangaroos.

A troop of 'roos invaded the track before the first race could get under way, but efforts to chase them away were foiled by what appeared almost to be a pre-planned tactic, as Racing Victoria steward Peter Ryan explained: 'Three separate waves of kangaroos came onto the course and left me with no choice but to terminate the seven-race card due to safety concerns.'

The course had had previous run-ins with the local kangaroos and constructed a large fence to foil them, but the animals outflanked the defences, firstly appearing around the back of the track to sneak in, and then jumping a smaller fence.

At one point, to raucous cheers from the crowd, a 'roo ran a finish down the home straight.

STARK CHOICE

In January 2011, Kempton racecourse boss Amy Starkey made headlines as she offered racing fans their money back for February's Racing Post Chase day – if the meeting turned out not to be exciting enough.

And how was that to be measured? Well, Amy commissioned 'biometric research' (no, me neither) which involved taking heart-rate, blood-flow and perspiration measurements (yes, okay, Amy) and apparently proved that horseracing generates more excitement and adrenalin rush than any other sport – and then she pledged that if a randomly-chosen ten volunteer racegoers monitored by, um, Mindlab International researchers throughout Racing Post day did not demonstrate sufficient levels of excitement, everyone would get their admission fee back.

They didn't.

The *Post* confirmed on the day after the race, run on 26 February, that 'several hundred racegoers' had signed up to get their money back if not enough thrills were forthcoming.

But, reported Jon Lees, University of Sussex scientists who monitored the requisite ten spectators 'found that the participants' heart-rates rose to an average peak of 109 beats per minute, with the top heart-rate recorded as 129bpm'.

CARR CRASH

Now a trainer, then a rider, Ruth Carr recalls a hot day at Cartmel racecourse in the Lake District: 'I was tailed off, and as I pulled up and hacked back the drunken crowd started pelting me with beer cans and doing donkey impressions.' Charming.

SCALPED AT THE SALES

An auctioneer was happy to have sold off a well-bred yearling filly for $1 million at the August 2009 Fasig-Tipton Saratoga Yearling Sale in New York.

The purchaser was a bald man, clad in a plaid shirt, sitting in the front row of seats, and after signing the sale ticket he walked off, snubbing reporters wanting to talk to him.

Anonymous bidders are not unknown at such sales but this man also refused to co-operate with Fasig-Tipton President, Boyd Browning, and then strode off, leaving behind him a stunned silence – and no money.

'I've never seen anything like this,' declared the yearling seller, Holly Bandoroff of Denali Stud, as police were called in.

'I'm told he was drunk, had no credit and has run away,' added Bandoroff – and that was just about the size of it.

Bandoroff recalled another odd sale event: 'I remember one year at Keeneland some lady was walking round with a scan of her brain, telling everybody she had had a lobotomy.'

The filly later went through the ring again, to be knocked down for $300,000.

HERE IS THE NUDES

Hesketh K. Naylor was reportedly a fan of cricket – but not the conventional variety.

Respected cricket writer David Rayvern Allen recorded how mid-nineteenth-century US millionaire Naylor 'kept an establishment of women with fuller figures to play cricket with balloons in the nude'.

Naylor did not participate but just observed as the matches unfolded.

TEETHING TROUBLES

When snooker ref Dave Oliver was requested during an Oxfordshire club match to clean the cue ball, he suddenly realised that he had no marker with which to mark the point on the green baize from which the ball would have to be lifted.

A spectator, Mick Fogarty, saw Oliver rummaging through his pockets and, reported writer Chris Rhys, in his 1986 book *Snooker Disasters and Bizarre Records*, eventually volunteering the loan of his bottom set of false teeth.

Like Cinderella's slipper, the teeth fitted the ball perfectly and were duly pressed into action.

NOT BEYOND OUR KEN

Arizona Diamondbacks owner Ken Kendrick forced fans of the Los Angeles Dodgers to change clothes or find a different seating location when the teams played in April 2013.

The fans, seated in a box suite costing over $3,000, were decked out in Dodgers blue when the game began.

But their colours soon changed: ushers were soon spotted conveying Diamondbacks gear to the suite, which the Dodgers fans had to change into if they wanted to keep their seats.

Here's the team's official explanation:

Due to the high visibility of the home plate box, we ask opposing team's fans when they purchase those seats to refrain from wearing that team's colours. During last night's game, when Ken Kendrick noticed the fans there, he offered them another suite if they preferred to remain in their Dodgers gear. When they chose to stay, he bought them all D-backs gear and a round of drinks and requested that they abide by our policy, and they obliged.

RODMAN'S LATEST KOREA MOVE

It emerged in March 2013 that basketball had a surprising fan: North Korean leader Kim Jong-Un.

And in one of the more bizarre juxtapositions of fan and hero, his basketball idol, the eccentric, controversial Dennis Rodman, was photographed sitting next to the leader at an exhibition basketball game in that country. North Korea's state TV channel, KRT, reported on the meeting of Kim Jong-Un and ex-Chicago Bulls star Rodman, who had arrived in the country to film a documentary with the Harlem Globetrotters. Kim and his wife watched the game with Rodman before attending a dinner in honour of their NBA guests.

CONNIE MAN?

Connie Mack was the manager of Philadelphia Athletics baseball club for a record-breaking fifty years, serving from 1901 to 1951. He had an easygoing managerial style – but the 'Tall Tactician' wouldn't stand for bad behaviour from the fans.

During a 1927 match, Mack became irate at a fan's persistent heckling of three players – Zack Wheat, Sammy Hale and, most intently, 'Bustin' Bill' Lamar.

Mack called in the police, who arrested the fan, one Harry Donnelly. Mack then attended Donnelly's hearing, where he accused the 26-year-old of causing players to make errors which resulted in them losing matches.

Donnelly was held on $500 bail for disturbing the peace – and a distressed Lamar never played again.

SKY'S THE LIMIT

When the New York Mets club complained that they felt their fans weren't getting behind them during the 1986 World Series against the Red Sox, Michael Sergio took it personally and decided to do something about it.

So the Emmy Award-winning actor parachuted into the Shea Stadium venue during the first inning of the sixth game, trailing behind his 'chute a banner proclaiming 'Let's Go Mets'.

After landing, Sergio high-fived pitcher Ron Darling, only to be nabbed by New York's finest and slung into a police van.

He later pleaded guilty to criminal trespass and reckless endangerment.

Still, the Mets were obviously inspired by Sergio: they won the game and clinched the series the next day.

GETTING THE UMP

The renowned Bill Klem – perhaps the Dickie Bird of his sport – claimed a unique distinction when in 1911 he became the first baseball umpire to dismiss a fan from an arena.

Chicago player Mordecai Brown was causing havoc among the home Philadelphia side when a fan began to slate him constantly.

Klem strode over to confront the man, telling him, 'Sir, you did not buy that seat to insult ball players.'

Responded the spectator, 'Go ump the game, you big fathead.'

Klem called the cops, who soon removed the fan from the ground.

WHEELY SHAPELY

Sheila Nicholls, described inevitably as 'shapely' by tabloids, ran onto the Lord's pitch as 25,000 fans watched a match between England and Australia in 1989. She was completely sober, and streaked because 'someone said it would be funny if there was a streaker, and suddenly I had this urge. I waited for the over to finish before going onto the pitch. It wouldn't be cricket to interrupt play.' Having escaped a number of police officers, she 'rounded it off with a cartwheel'. Led from the field into the pavilion, the Australian players wanted to shake her hand, and 'a big fat chap with an MCC tie strode up to me and said, "Jolly well done." That made me feel much better.' She was cautioned for disorderly behaviour.

SAM THE OUTSIDER

Ledbury Town FC fan Sam Phillips was banned from his favourite club's ground after being accused of assaulting the referee during a 1980 match.

Nothing that remarkable about an incident of that nature at a football ground – except that Sam was in his eighties at the time.

Nor was he prepared to give up his team without a struggle – he turned up outside the ground and watched through a hedge behind the pitch.

BUM DEAL

Racing UK viewers were not impressed when the last race shown on the channel from Beverley's evening meeting on 30 May 2007 was accompanied by the unedifying sight of the bared rear end of a presumably inebriated racegoer, perched on a stool near the rails, aimed at the cameras, as the runners headed into the final four furlongs. Still worse was the fact that the bum pictures were still being shown the next day as replays of the meeting's races were broadcast.

TAKING THE MIKE

Ranelagh Harriers runner Mike Peace, who has run the race over thirty times, was heading down the Mall to the finishing line in the London Marathon, when suddenly, a spectator rushed into the middle of the road in front of him, planting a kiss on the startled runner.

The woman was rapidly grabbed by pursuing police and dragged off for questioning.

It was Mike Peace's mother, Christine.

KEEPING MUM

Cleveland Indians pitcher Bob Feller knew his parents had travelled from Iowa to watch him pitch in Chicago against the White Sox on Mother's Day 1939. So he must have felt a flicker of anxiety when Chicago batter Marv Owen hit a shot sending the ball into the crowd – and he was right to be anxious. The ball hit Feller's mother in the face, smashing her spectacles and opening a cut which required stitches.

Feller was allowed time to go into the stand to check on his mother, returning to the pitch to strike Owen out, winning the game.

GNATS THE WAY

One of the most bizarre reasons for concluding a sporting contest prematurely occurred on 15 September 1946, when fans at the Chicago Cubs versus Brooklyn Dodgers game began waving their white scorecards in a frantic effort to disperse an infestation of gnats which had descended on Ebbets Field during the sixth inning of a match the Dodgers were winning 2–0.

With bright sun shining and the scorecards dazzling as they flapped, it was ruled that there was 'a hazard to the players' vision', and the match was curtailed at that point.

STAN COLLY-MURDER?

Dominic Hourd, a Newcastle fan, accused then Liverpool player Stan Collymore of causing the death of his pet budgerigar.

After Collymore scored a late winner as Newcastle lost to Liverpool in 1996, Hourd, watching at home, kicked out in frustration, knocking his budgie's cage off its stand, causing the bird's demise.

'Collymore can't bring Peter the Budgie back, but I told him I couldn't forgive him for what he did,' said Hourd, who wrote to Collymore to explain the unexpected consequence of his goal-scoring action.

EXTRA TIME

Celtic supporter Harry Moin actually died during a 1999 match, when the 42-year-old suffered a heart attack and was declared technically dead, before being revived three minutes later.

FAN-TASTIC QUOTES

'Most people are in a factory from nine till five. Their job may be to turn out 263 circles. At the end of the week they're three short and somebody has a go at them. On Saturday afternoons they deserve something to go and shout about.'

  – Rodney Marsh, footballer turned pundit, 1969.

'Certain fans need to not come and support this team ... Coming out to BOO us ... Stay at home ... Don't need ur BOO's ... SAY NO MORE!!!!'

  – Newcastle player Nile Ranger's Twitter advice to supporters, following January 2013 defeat to lowly Reading.

'It's easy to blame money, so let's do just that ... Players and managers now seem to operate with little concept of duty and responsibility and the moral boundaries of barbarians. They don't have to think of anyone else so they don't. And this sets an example to the fans.'

  – Roger Alton, *The Spectator*, October 2012.

'Edgbaston was awash with social inadequates, bawling, brawling, caterwauling; slating, baiting, hating … a cave of sullen youths, for whom insolence, ugliness and selfishness are basic facts of life.'

– Michael Henderson of *The Times* on a Test crowd in 1998.

'Without the fans, a stadium is just another building on another street.'

– Henry Winter, *Sunday Telegraph*, 20 January 2013.

'Never is a man more feminine than when it comes to football. Show me a fan and I will show you a woman's brain dressed in a polyester shirt.'

– Helen Rumbelow, *The Times*, 16 August 2007

'To walk onto the turf of the team you've supported all your life is like climbing into the telly or being given the keys to Wonka's chocolate factory.'

– Russell Brand, delighted at being invited onto the West Ham pitch by Christian Dailly, 18 August 2007.

Sky Sports reporter: 'Why are you travelling to Southampton on a Monday night?!'

Everton fan: 'Because of you lot.'

– Sky Sports, 21 January 2013.

'Our hearts begin to beat with healthy, sporting tension as soon as the referee's whistle blows, sounding like the first bird of spring, as soon as the first moves are made on the green field.'

– Soviet writer Lev Filatov, waxing lyrical about fans' feelings in March 1957.

DEAD LOSS

Widow Wendy Moss arranged for her Leeds United fan husband Nigel's remains to be buried at Elland Road in August 2001.

However, when the box containing Nigel's ashes was opened it was empty. Co-op Funeral Services were unable to explain where they had gone.

HITTING THE MARK

Irked at being roundly abused by Reading fans, Bristol City defender Gerard Lavin kicked the ball hard at an advertising board during a Division Two game in August 1999, only to miss and hit Reading supporter Mark Steven, breaking his wrist.

CORNERED IN BED

Huddersfield fan David Tagg had been bedridden through illness for eight years but was longing to see his club play again.

So in 1969 nineteen-year-old David was collected, along with his bed, from his hospital by a removal van paid for by the club – and taken to see Huddersfield take on Blackpool and beat them 2–0.

David and his bed were deposited very close to one of the corner flags, from which position he cheered his heroes on to victory.

PEDALLING PEDRO

Pedro Garita cycled from Buenos Aires to Mexico City to see the 1986 World Cup final – only to discover on arrival that he could not afford to pay for a ticket.

What's more, when the gloomy 52-year-old returned from the ticket office he found his bike had been stolen.

DECENT SHOT

A football fan was jailed for two months in February 1999 in Reims, France, after he stopped the opposition scoring – by shooting the goal-bound ball with his revolver.

REALLY?!

A Real Madrid fan had to take his favourite club to court to have a nine-month ban and £3 fine lifted in 1962.

His dastardly crime? Applauding when the opposition scored, which offence had produced a letter from the club reminding him: 'You must not encourage our opponents.'

GANGLING STRIKER

Southampton legend Matt Le Tissier, often referred to as 'Le God' by fans, was also credited with healing powers by supporter Rebecca Malthouse, who was watching him play in a May 1998 game.

Le Tissier hit a wayward shot which struck Rebecca, who was sitting behind the goal, on her hand – removing a fluid-filled ganglion which was due to be operated on shortly afterwards.

TOO POMPED UP

Extreme Portsmouth fan John Portsmouth Football Club Westwood, who changed his name by deed poll (you don't say!), was presented with a long-service loyalty award by the club prior to their December 1998 match against Grimsby.

The match was marred when a fan ran onto the pitch after the game. He was subsequently banned from the ground for life.

It was John Portsmouth Football Club Westwood.

GIVE US A RING, PLEASE

Norwich fan John Jordan was somewhat surprised to discover a wedding ring in his shoe when he returned home from a December 1999 game against QPR.

He rang the club, and discovered that it belonged to Diane Thirkettle, a fellow supporter, who had lost it while applauding during the game – and had already given it up as lost.

MARK MY WORDS

Sports fan Mark Roberts made a name for himself as a serial streaker after racking up an incredible number of appearances at events both sporting and other, including the Ryder Cup, the Winter Olympics and the Ashes.

At last count, his scorecard listed well over 500 streaks, and featured venues as diverse as racecourses, tennis matches, synchronised swimming championships, both Mr Universe and Miss World contests, the bull run in Pamplona and – his speciality – football matches.

A father of three, Roberts's 'career' began when he saw a female streaker run naked onto the pitch during a 1993 Rugby Sevens game in Hong Kong. Spurred on by the sight – and by encouragement from his friends in the form of a drunken bet – he went naked in front of the crowd himself the very next day, and evidently enjoyed the experience.

Since then, Roberts has become so well known for his exploits that he is regularly required to hand over his passport before attending an event, to assuage the organisers' fears about a potential spectacle.

And he burst into the consciousness of those immune to sport in 1995, when he gatecrashed a live broadcast of *This Morning*, where he swam onto presenter Fred Talbot's floating weather map and proceeded to emulate Talbot's trademark leap from Scotland to Ireland.

But he was somewhat upstaged at 2004's Super Bowl in Houston, Texas, where his uncharacteristically modest performance, which saw him dancing in a thong, was surpassed by Janet Jackson's half-time show.

Unlike Jackson, however, Roberts was tackled by members of the New England Patriots (whose linebacker

Matt Chatham grabbed him) and Carolina Panthers, as well as by police and security, and was taken into custody. He was later fined $1,000 for trespassing.

'Janet Jackson was wearing the nipple clamp and I'm the one who got arrested?' says Roberts, who has been fined some £10,000 in total since he started streaking.

He successfully streaked at Royal Ascot on Ladies Day, 19 June 2003. He performed his streak shortly before the main race of the day, appearing as 'Lady Muck', stripping out of a full-length black batwing dress.

During the World Snooker final in 2004 between Ronnie O'Sullivan and Graeme Dott, he ran down the stairs and tried to claim asylum under the table.

Roberts had planned on retiring with one last streak at the 2006 World Cup final in Germany, but was thwarted when he was stopped before entering the stadium.

However, in that year at the 2006 Winter Olympics, the serial stripper interrupted the men's bronze medal curling match between the US and UK, wearing nothing but a strategically placed rubber chicken, and in 2010 he continued the animal theme by appearing at Crufts dog show sporting a cat-shaped mask over his privates.

Roberts turned pro in 2011, when artist Benedikt Dichgans hired him to streak in Tate Britain and at the Turner Prize, though the gig was not entirely without hiccups, ending as it did in Roberts's arrest.

Towards the end of 2012, Roberts was planning yet another farewell performance of the streaking art and on his website, www.thestreaker.org.uk, he explained: 'Men and women of every colour, nationality, shape and size are invited to take part in Mark Roberts's last streaking performance. The Mass Streak, scheduled some time in the coming months, will hopefully involve hundreds if not thousands of streakers.'

Roberts has also been advertising for a ghost-writer to help with his planned biography.

I didn't volunteer.

In February 2013, Roberts, who by then claimed 517 life-time streaks, was the subject of a Channel 4 TV documentary, *Streak! The Man Who Can't Keep His Clothes On*, in which, rather unexpectedly, he was shown changing his mind about performing one final streak before retiring, for the TV cameras.

That's about the bare bones of the man who so regularly made the nudes.

NO ONE CARED

The official fan attendance for Bradford City's 2–0 win over Norwich on 3 March 1915 was: none.

In a similar vein, Houston Astros were ready to play

Pittsburgh Pirates on 15 June 1976 but after 10 inches of rain had fallen there were no fans, no umpires and no stadium personnel at the Houston Astrodome. The Americans obviously weren't made of such stern stuff, though – they opted not to bother playing in the absence of spectators.

DRIVEN MAD BY FAN PROTEST

David Coulthard, still in with a fair chance of winning the 2000 World Drivers' Championship in which he was just six points behind leader Michael Schumacher, was poised in second place behind Mika Hakkinen as they set out on the twenty-fourth lap of the German Grand Prix.

Driving for McLaren-Mercedes, Coulthard was shocked to see a spectator suddenly appear on the Hockenheim circuit. The fan had found a way through the fences before running across the track near the Clark Kurve and then setting off walking along a grass verge.

Race organisers immediately summoned the safety car to come out until the security guards could get to the intruder.

At this point Hakkinen suddenly nipped off the track to pit, anticipating the safety car. Coulthard had been planning to pit on this lap, but when he saw Hakkinen go he decided to stay out – but, crucially, was not expecting the arrival of the safety car.

So, once the safety car had slowed the drivers right down for three laps, Hakkinen was back out, with Coulthard having had to sit and suffer in silence until he could finally get into the pits, from where he emerged in sixth place, eventually coming home in third place rather than keeping title hopes alive with a win.

Commented McLaren's Ron Dennis: 'We had flexibility in our strategy, but not sufficient to accommodate a deranged spectator, who wandered onto the circuit, costing us the race and endangering his and the lives of the drivers.'

It transpired that the spectator who had come onto the track was a 47-year-old Frenchman who had recently been dismissed from his job with – ironically – Mercedes-Benz and who was, albeit only in his own mind, making a protest in this irresponsible manner.

STAT'S THE WAY TO DO IT

Angus Loughran shot to fame as the geeky football fount of knowledge on the BBC TV show *Fantasy Football*.

He later became the betting expert during the channel's

racing coverage. His own betting began at Ampleforth, the Catholic school he attended in Yorkshire, where he would offer odds about how many monks would turn up each week for Sunday mass – but his gambling career would eventually result in him gatecrashing a major sporting contest.

It happened in 1982 (at which time he was just fifteen), when he was sitting at the Oval cricket ground watching Chris Tavare batting – very slowly – for England against India. Bored by the lack of on-pitch action, Loughran began to take bets from fellow spectators that he would take a stool out to the wicket and sit on it while the game was in progress.

When he stood to win £300 by sitting, Loughran took the precaution of mentioning to India's boundary fielder Kapil Dev what he was about to do, then sauntered onto the outfield and made his way to the wicket, clutching the stool, before sitting on it to win the wagers – and promptly being arrested.

THREATENING BEHAVIOUR

On 15 September 1981, the media revealed Bjorn Borg's chances of winning the US Open were dashed after being the subject of a death threat received by New York

Police, who were told by a caller that he would 'kill Borg when he walked on the court'. He lost to McEnroe in four sets. In 1980 Borg had been fined £23,000 for cancelling an exhibition match, also against McEnroe, for similar reasons.

Defiant in the face of threats, Kevin Keegan played for England in a 0–0 draw against Northern Ireland in Belfast in 1975, despite having been told by the FA that they had received a threat to shoot him if he played. 'I am not going to let an anonymous nutter stop me just because I have Irish ancestry,' declared Keegan, who got a great reception from the crowd – but four days later Don Revie dropped him from the next game, against Wales.

JOCKED OFF

Racing fans came to the rescue of jockey Willie Carson, who was pulled from his horse by striking stable lads demonstrating in pursuit of a pay rise, on the way down to the start of the 1,000 Guineas Classic race at Newmarket in May 1981.

Spectators rushed to his rescue, protecting Carson and fellow jockeys who appeared to be in danger.

WHISTLE-STOP GOAL

Derby defenders came to a standstill when a fan blew a whistle during their 1986 game against Aston Villa. Villa forward Tony Daley, however, ignored the false whistler to score and equalise. The incident controversially put Villa through to the next round of the League Cup, as they won the replay.

HAVE MERCI

As the 1924 Olympic rugby union final between France and the USA took place in Paris, French fans booed and hissed the Americans after their star player, Adolphe Jauréguy, was flattened by a hard tackle just two minutes after the game began, leaving him unconscious with blood pouring down his face.

In the second half, French fans hurled bottles and rocks onto the pitch, and also at US players and officials. Brawls broke out in the stands, US reserve Gideon Nelson was knocked unconscious after being hit in the face by a walking stick, and French fans invaded the pitch at the final whistle, leaving the French team, aided by the police, to attempt to protect the Americans.

At the medal ceremony, 'The Star Spangled Banner'

was drowned out by the booing and hissing of French fans, and the American team had to be escorted to the dressing room under police protection. The Americans remain Olympic champions, as the sport has not been represented at the Games since, though it is set to return in 2016.

J. LOW'S PILGRIMAGE

Scotland fan John Low travelled 7,350 miles from his home in Castle Douglas to Mendoza, Argentina, in June 2008, so that he could recreate one of Scotland's most famous football moments thirty years on to the day.

John, in his fifties, recruited Argentinian office workers to act as Dutch defenders so that he could play out the role of Archie Gemmill, who scored a remarkable goal against Holland during the 1978 World Cup at the Estadio Malvinas.

I just turned up on the day. I managed to track down the woman who was director of the sports complex – and she was suitably impressed by me wearing a kilt. All the people who worked in the stadium viewed me as a bit of an oddity. I needed people to be the Dutch defenders and goalie. I managed to persuade a few office workers.

John donned a replica Scotland kit to reproduce the goal – and, while he was doing so, bumped into fellow Castle Douglas resident Jim Kentley, who had gone out for the World Cup in 1978 and liked the place so much he never went home.

A REICH COCK-UP

Supporters watching on giant screens booed and threw beer and food, and complaints poured into the station as, prior to the Euro 2008 finals match between Germany and Austria, the Swiss TV broadcaster SRG displayed the words to the German national anthem.

However, they had put up the words to the song's first stanza, which was banned after the Second World War: 'Deutschland, Deutschland über alles, über alles in der Welt'.

TUNNEL VISION

In despair at not being able to get tickets for a Champions League match, Galatasaray fans took matters into their own hands in March 2013 – quite literally. Horst Heldt, sporting director of Galatasary's opponents, Schalke, told reporters that they had found a group of supporters trying to burrow their way into their stadium.

The ground around the perimeter fence was frozen solid, but that wasn't enough to deter the would-be spectators. With the away section sold out and tickets trading hands at inflated prices, the group resorted to desperate measures, attempting to dig a tunnel with their bare hands.

The Turkish side ended up winning 4–3 on aggregate – perhaps spurred on to victory by the true fanaticism of their supporters.

BROLLY GOOD

In his book *40 Years in Football*, published in the 1950s, Ivan Sharpe recalled how, during a vital Second Division football match between promotion-chasing West Ham and Notts County in May 1923, 'a woman ran onto the field and assaulted County keeper Albert Iremonger with her umbrella because he was threatening to stand between United and promotion'.

The Hammers lost that game, but did go up.

Coming a little more up to date, another fan with a brolly, this time male – the fan, that is – attacked Bayern Munich star Sepp Maier after their December

1968 match at Hanover, whereupon Franz 'Der Kaiser' Beckenbauer, regarded by most Brits as the greatest of German players, punched the assailant to the ground.

As a result, Maier was later fined 1,000 Deutschmarks because he 'provoked the crowd' – which, indeed, is not an unreasonable reading of his pretending to urinate at Hanover fans.

KNOCK OUT

The New York Yankees were trailing the Orioles 4–3 in the eighth inning of the first game of the 1996 American League Championship Series at Yankee Stadium.

Yankee star player Derek Jeter hit a ball to deep right. Orioles right-fielder Tony Tarasco drifted back, but as he reached up in an effort to catch the ball, a twelve-year-old from New Jersey named Jeffrey Maier reached over the fence and knocked the ball back into the stands. Umpire Rich Garcia declared a home run, levelling the score.

The Yankees went on to win 5–4. An Orioles protest was dismissed because 'judgement calls cannot be protested'. After reviewing the tape, Garcia accepted that Maier did reach over the fence but added that he didn't believe Tarasco would have made the catch.

The Yankees won the series in five games, then defeated the Braves in six games to win their first World Series since 1978.

Next season, Yankee Stadium erected a railing to prevent fans from reaching over the fence. Maier became something of a celebrity, appearing on David Letterman's TV show, and was given a key to the city by New York mayor Rudy Giuliani.

PANT-ASTIC

'We started brilliantly, but this pants thing destroyed us,' was the bizarre comment by Reading manager Alan Pardew after his side failed to beat Wrexham in their December 1999 2–2 Division Two draw.

Pardew declined to comment on the fact that his chairman, John Madejski, had reportedly joined in with the estimated several thousand Reading fans who had made known their displeasure over recent poor performances by waving pairs of underpants around.

For a, ahem, brief spell, the pants were really whirling as Reading fell 1–2 behind, having taken the lead.

The campaign had begun on a Reading fans website, and the 'PANTS' theme arose to indicate the fans' belief that 'Players Are Not Trying Sufficiently'.

REVVED UP

Inter Milan's hardcore, 'curva' fans excelled themselves during a 2002 game against Atalanta when, despite stewards being out in force, they managed somehow to smuggle a *motorbike* into the second tier of the stadium – a motorbike whose licence plates reportedly emanated from the Atalanta area.

Once the vehicle had emerged, a group of the fans battered it to within an inch of its motorised life, before pushing it over the edge of the barrier and, probably before the very eyes of its appalled owner, sending it crashing to the – fortunately empty – terraces below.

I'M OUT OF HERE

When 31-year-old Arminia Bielefeld keeper Goran Ćurko slipped and almost conceded an own goal during an October 2000 German second-division match against Waldhof Mannheim, his own fans turned on him, chanting, 'Ćurko out … Ćurko out…'

So, Ćurko went. To the astonishment of the crowd, the player just walked straight off the pitch, acquiring a yellow card en route from the bemused ref.

And he just kept on walking, straight into the dressing

room, having to be replaced by young sub Dennis Eilhoff – who went on to keep a clean sheet.

'I was simply not able to continue playing,' was the closest Ćurko came to explaining his actions.

SPAT WITH A FAN

Wolverhampton Wanderers manager Graham Taylor not unnaturally took offence when a fan spat at him following the team's April 1995 3–3 draw at Sheffield United.

Taylor attempted unsuccessfully to make a citizen's arrest at the time, but four days later Blades fan Robert Hollister admitted to the offence and, following his release on bail, travelled to Molineux to apologise personally to Taylor.

PEÑAROL PELT

Peñarol fans were not best pleased that their side were trailing Danubio in a Uruguayan League match in June 1996 by a goal to nil. The fans began to pelt the pitch with rocks, bottles, coins and any number of objects in an effort to have the game abandoned.

The ref initially refused to submit to the blackmail by barrage, but when he saw his linesman lying flat out, having been felled by a motorcycle helmet, he admitted defeat and called the game off.

THAT'S 'ANDY

Newly appointed Secretary of State for Culture, Media and Sport, Andy Burnham, who took office in February 2008, decided he had better make a clean breast of his murky past as a hooligan fan, so admitted, 'I invaded the pitch when Everton's Adrian Heath got his last-minute winner at Highbury.'

Burnham was, however, fourteen years old at the time.

Asked by *Independent* reader Kevin O'Neill of Liverpool whether he thought that fans 'who run on the pitch should be given a lifetime ban', Burnham responded, 'I think there should be second chances for young lads, particularly Evertonians, who take part in good-natured pitch celebrations when they have suffered a childhood of disappointment up to that point.'

BARELY WORTH IT?

The excitement of seeing Blackpool take a 2–1 lead at Torquay in August 2000 prompted a fan to streak in celebration, delaying the match for four minutes.

During the time added on for his ill-advised strip show, Torquay rallied to score twice, winning 3–2.

WE'RE CROSS FANS

Macedonian side Vardar Skopje were left in no doubt as to the feelings of the fans who marked their elimination from the UEFA Cup by a side from Cyprus in the early stages of the 2007–08 season by digging a grave overnight in the middle of their stadium and leaving behind a cross bearing the message 'RIP 2007 Uprava (management)'.

Their coach, Dragi Kanatlarovski, was duly fired.

SOX IT TO 'EM

The fan who wrote to the Chicago White Sox demanding an autographed baseball 'or I will never watch you again' obviously expected his emotional blackmail to pay off.

So he must have been nonplussed when, in June 1995, the club's marketing vice-president, Rob Gallas, wrote back to Mr Michael Robelli:

We receive thousands of letters every year from all over the country. Many are outrageous. Congratulations! Your letter made it to the top of the list.

So, you want an autographed ball and you will return to baseball. Please do us a favour. Stay away. We are going to be doing a lot [of things] for our fans, but bribery isn't one of them.

GUNNING FOR THE REF

The ref sent a player off during a 1974 Sicilian league match in Syracuse. 'So what?' I hear you cry.

But one home fan was far from stoic about the decision; so disappointed was he that he discharged his double-barrelled hunting gun, then suggested that the ref might wish to reconsider his decision.

He did. The player returned and Syracuse duly won – by seven goals.

REF RUCTIONS

After the 1923 title fight in Georgia, USA, between holder Mike McTigue and challenger 'Young' Stribling was declared a draw by Harry Ertle, the referee was immediately surrounded by a hostile mob of furious Stribling fans who 'persuaded' the official to amend the verdict to victory for their man.

Ertle did so – but once the ring was cleared he telephoned press representatives to inform them that he was reinstating his original verdict of a draw.

Stribling's three-hour reign as World Light Heavyweight Champion was over.

FAN-TOM PLAYERS

Fans of American football turned up in their droves to watch a highly rated crack German side based in Munich take on their local heroes, Sheffield Great Britain Spartans, in a May 1995 international challenge match.

But after the highly touted visitors were thrashed 108–62, irate fans demanded their money back, accusing the match organisers of duping them.

Some observant Sheffield fans had recognised one of their team's reserve players clad in Munich kit.

They were even more astonished to discover that virtually the entire 'German' side was made up of Sheffield second-string players and that only three of the Munich line-up were real Germans.

As protests mounted, Terry Smith, Spartans manager and club owner, was eventually forced to hand back spectators' entrance money or offer them free tickets for three future matches.

Smith claimed that six Munich players had arrived for the fixture, but that 'faced with a shortfall of Munich players I had no alternative but to supplement the German side, or call the game off, which would have caused more disappointment'.

One Sheffield fan who had seen and heard the 'Germans' proudly listening to or singing their national anthem pre-match commented, 'I feel let down – we were wildly clapping our own side but in fact we were being duped.'

WATER TORTURE

Tour de France fans often rush up the course following – and often touching or impeding – the riders. Usually any damage to a rider's chances is accidental, although the possibility of deliberate sabotage remains.

Fans were blamed by two Italian teams during the 1950 Tour after rider Gino Bartali was 'harassed' on the Col d'Aspin and quit, claiming he had been threatened by a knife-wielding fan.

In 1966 a spectator threw a bucket of water over rider Jacques Anquetil on the Grand St-Bernard, perhaps seeking to refresh him.

Instead, by the time the rider reached the bottom of the descent he was frozen and struggling to breathe; he quit the race the next day.

Legendary rider Eddy Merckx was punched while on the Puy-de-Dome by a race fan.

Thirty-year-old actor Xavier Clement streaked as the riders in the 1975 Tour were on the Champs Elysees – he was fined the equivalent of £210 for 'sexual exhibition' but won the free lunch bet he'd struck beforehand.

Cycling writer William Fotheringham recalls a fan 'dressed as Jesus who waved at us from a cross in the Perigord'.

CLOUGH AND NONSENSE AS 'S**T HITS FAN'

Brian Clough nurtured his own reputation for eccentricity. But later in his career he also suffered health problems which may have affected his actions.

However, the last thing any Nottingham Forest fans would have anticipated as they joyfully invaded the pitch after beating QPR 5–2 was being punched by their team's boss.

But as a search of YouTube will reveal, that is exactly what happened during the 1989 match, with three supporters feeling the force of Clough's fists in an extraordinary overreaction to the situation.

Eventually, Clough made a public apology to two of them on TV, during the course of which he spoke to the men as if they were errant children, before bizarrely insisting that they both kiss him.

A local television journalist recalled: 'On BBC *Midlands Today*, we saw the cut story in which Clough made the two young men kiss him – as a way of saying he forgave them.

'It all appeared jovial and forgiving but when the three first met it was prickly to say the least.'

Clough was fined £5,000 by the FA.

The incident was also immortalised by tabloid papers with the comment that this was the 'first televised case of the s**t hitting the fan'!

In September 1978 Clough had threatened to close off parts of the ground where supporters had been making obscene chants against opponents. 'They are making me sick. If they don't cut it out we'll shift them out,' he vowed. In 1986 he aimed a 'V' sign at Forest fans cheering at an injured opponent being stretchered off.

BARMY FANS

Now known the world over for following England's cricket team around the world, the conglomeration of fans known as the Barmy Army is a true fan phenomenon which even boasts its own website, www.barmyarmy.com.

The Barmy Army has become the UK's largest and most successful organisation aimed at helping cricket fans watch and support the England cricket team play all over the world. In addition, the Barmy Army also now organises cricket tours, provides match-day tickets and merchandising, and runs a very successful membership scheme.

Started by three friends on the 1994–95 Ashes tour, the Barmy Army, which now has over 5,000 members, has been supporting England's cricket team all over the world ever since, bringing its unique carnival atmosphere to the game.

Many, though, have mixed feelings about the BA – the late cricket writer Christopher Martin-Jenkins once accused them of 'demeaning cricket', and although many grounds set aside specific areas for members, at Lord's they are banned.

Mail on Sunday columnist Patrick Collins dismisses them as 'dreary grotesques'.

The Barmy Army, which is a limited company, claims it wants to 'make watching cricket more fun and much more popular'. The group uses flags, banners, songs and chants to inspire the team and to encourage crowd participation in their activities. In contrast to the reputations of some sports fans for hooliganism, the Barmy Army organisers actively discourage unsavoury behaviour.

The group engages in charity work, and has a good reputation among cricket administrators and among some other fans. However, some cricket followers find the chanting of the Barmy Army to be annoying, lowbrow and disruptive.

Barney Ronay made his views obvious in a 2006 *Guardian* blog:

It's not as though we haven't seen it all before: large, sunburnt men attempt a slow-motion conga; someone waves a crumpled flag; depressed-looking people in funny costumes suddenly wake up and start punching the air on catching a glimpse of themselves on the big screen; and, yes, here he is again, Victor 'Jimmy' Flowers, leader of the Barmy Army, also known as that skinny bloke in the singlet with the stringy blonde highlights who keeps jumping around, drawing attention to himself and not really paying any attention to the cricket.

Annoyingly, the Army has begun to make its own headlines. It threatened to boycott the rest of the series after rough treatment at The Gabba. Pockets of supporters were discouraged. A trumpeter was ejected. 'Everything is geared to try and make sure there is no fun in the game,' said Army spokesman Paul Burnham. What fun could there possibly be at the first Test of a titanic Ashes series without a trumpet? A Cricket Australia spokesman said they were just targeting 'a small minority of idiots who have been ruining people's day out at the cricket for some time'. Which, whisper it, sounds about right.

Originally, 'Barmy Army' was a repetitive football chant sung by fans at many grounds, including Norwich City in the late 1970s and Sheffield Wednesday in the early 1980s. In conjunction with the increasing appearance of English football shirts at cricket grounds in the early 1990s, the song's repetitive cry of 'Barmy Army, Barmy Army, Barmy Army' transferred to domestic cricket arenas at Old Trafford and Headingley.

Throughout the 1990s, increased spending power

enabled fans to take the song overseas when following tours of the English national cricket team. Because of that particular song, and the fact that it seemed to represent English fans' activity of standing in the hot sun drinking lager all day, it became a description as well as a song. David Lloyd and Ian Botham used the tag to describe the supporters while commentating for Sky Sports during England's tours from 1993 to 1995.

Only in the mid-1990s was the tag recognised as an official title for English touring cricket fans and adopted by what is now recognised as the official Barmy Army.

ARGY BARGY

Argentinian racing fan Victor Rosales went to the races in Buenos Aires in 1990. He had a feeling 12/1 chance Broncaro was going to win.

And so sure was he of victory, he staked the equivalent of £10,000 on the horse.

Rosales watched as the three-year-old came out of the stalls, watched as the horse struggled to match strides with his opponents, watched as it finished stone last, watched the horse come back in from the course.

Rosales pulled out a revolver and shot … the horse.

BOWLED OVER BY THE FANS

Large crowds of fans would turn up to see district cricket matches in Sydney pre-World War Two, and one of the most notorious band of fans were the Marrickville 'Hill', who could get at opposition players but who in February 1932 excelled themselves by taking the credit for the dismissal of Randwick and New South Wales batsman Dr E. P. Barbour.

A book about the club, *History of Marrickville*, reported that 'Barbour usually had no problem in dealing with barrackers, but was disconcerted by a section of the crowd who were silent as the bowler ran in but who shouted "Hit it!" just after the ball left the bowler's hand.'

He appealed to the umpire and home captain, but no action resulted.

When the barracking continued, Barbour stepped away from his wicket just after the ball was delivered, and was bowled.

Barbour remained at the wicket for a minute discussing the matter with the umpire.

The scorecard read 'b. Amos', but it could have read 'b. Marrickville barrackers'.

FANKS A LOT

Derek McGovern, sports betting writer for the *Daily Mirror*, told in November 2006 how

a mate was in Zagreb with two Croatian pals the previous month to watch the England game. Urged by the two Croats to back Niko Kranjčar to score the first goal, he duly stuck £30 on at 12/1.

Portsmouth midfielder Kranjčar had three great chances and fluffed them all, much to the mate's disgust.

Two hours later, who should turn up at the same bar as the mate and his two Croatian buddies but Kranjčar himself.

Told about the bet his lousy finishing had scuppered, Kranjčar offered to pay out the winnings himself.

FANTOM OF THE SLOPES?

Jean-Claude Killy of France was the golden boy of the 1968 Winter Olympic Games in Grenoble-Chamrousse, and he went into the slalom event expected to win a triple crown of gold medals. The only threat to him was reckoned to come from Karl Schranz of Austria.

Killy had already completed his run in the gloom of a

foggy, misty day as Schranz prepared for his turn. What occurred next became one of the greatest controversies of the Games.

As Schranz skied towards the twenty-first gate of the course, he claimed a 'mysterious figure in black crossed the course'.

Schranz came to a halt and, with three 'witnesses' accompanying him, he returned to the start point and requested a rerun.

British referee Colonel Robert Redhead acceded to the request and, second time down, Schranz shredded the course and beat Killy's time – it seemed the gold medal was his, and he duly gave a celebratory press conference, much to Killy's displeasure.

However, Schranz's golden moment was short-lived and two hours later came an official statement, handing the gold to Killy and sensationally explaining that Schranz had been disqualified for missing out two gates, even before the mystery man/fan had appeared in front of him.

Schranz declared that if he had missed a gate it was because he had already been spooked by the phantom interloper. Those on his side now suggested that the mystery man may have been a French fan of Killy out to stop anyone depriving him of gold – perhaps a French soldier or policeman.

Killy's crowd hinted there had been no mystery fan at all. No one apparently suggested it was a wraith, a spectre of the slopes, or a ghostly ski entity.

Eventually the matter went to a Jury of Appeal meeting. The verdict was 3–1 in favour of Killy with one abstention – the referee, Col. Redhead.

SAY A LITTLE PRAYER

Former Hull striker Jozy Altidore said he would pray for fans who racially abused him during his Dutch side AZ Alkmaar's 5–0 victory at Den Bosch in January 2013.

Altidore, who scored one of AZ's goals, was targeted in the first half. The game was stopped by the referee, but the player asked that it should carry on.

'It's disappointing these things still happen in this time we're in, but what are you going to do?' said Altidore. 'You just hope that these people can improve themselves. You pray for them.'

I JUST KAHN'T BELIEVE THIS

Two Uzbekistan football fans were so determined to get the autograph of their idol, German goalkeeper

Oliver Khan, that in March 2006 Akram Marufshonow and Musadshon Chornidow cycled 4,000 miles across Europe from Tashkent to Berlin, where a German journalist heard of their quest and introduced them to their hero. Khan told them, 'I just can't believe this,' and duly supplied autographs for them.

LOYAL SUPPORT

Wendy Simpson and her dog Sammy, a collie, followed Newcastle during the '80s, '90s and 2000s, never missing a home game, travelling to many away grounds but only ever seeing one match – and that a testimonial for Peter Beardsley. For Wendy chauffeured son Ian to games from the age of ten, waiting in the various car parks for him to return after the matches.

POST-FAN

Hartlepool postman John Dawson was a fan of all football in the Northern League – where, during one season in the 1990s, he watched a record 270 games in one season. How many letters he had time to deliver is not recorded.

BOOTED OUT

Former Woolwich Arsenal footballer Bob Benson turned up as a fan to watch them play Reading in a 1916 wartime game.

Bob, 33, was persuaded to put his boots on and turn from fan back to player – which he agreed to do despite not having played since his retirement over two seasons earlier.

It was a fatal decision: his lack of fitness told, and he was helped from the pitch in clear distress, dying in the dressing room minutes later.

He was buried in an Arsenal shirt.

NET RESULT

A teenage ice hockey fan, Brittanie Cecil, died in 2002 after being hit by a puck during a match between the Columbus Blue Jackets and the Calgary Flames. Following the incident it became mandatory in the NHL to have protective netting above the glass and behind the goals.

JET READY

A 2013 Group C African Nations Cup match in Nelspruit between holders Zambia and Ethiopia descended into near-chaos, with angry Ethiopian fans throwing bottles and vuvuzelas onto the pitch when their keeper was sent off. The game ended 1–1. There was possibly a slight overreaction when, just to add to the mayhem, a jet fighter buzzed the stadium before order was finally restored.

KICKING OFF

In 2013, Wycombe keeper Jordan Archer suffered an attack from a violent yob running onto the pitch. Archer, 19, on loan from Spurs, was preparing to take a goal kick in the dying minutes of the League Two match at Gillingham when he was floored by a young thug who jumped on his back before stewards dragged him away.

JUST A MINUTE

The final sixty seconds of the Third Division game between Birmingham and Stoke in 1992 were played behind closed doors after the ground was cleared following a pitch invasion during which referee Roger Wiseman was hit by a fan. Wiseman subsequently withdrew from the list of Football League officials, citing 'mental stress' as the reason.

FAN-TASTIC QUOTES

'After a victory by our favourite team we fans are in a much better mood. You feel as hardy and healthy as if you had taken part in the game yourself. Our work goes well. But if you see a game in which your team plays a weak opponent and does poorly, all the time at work you are thinking about why they played so badly.'

– Tell me about it! June 1959 comments by anonymous Soviet-era engineer reported in *Sovetskii Sport*.

'When I go out on a mission, I don't know if I'm coming back but I'm committed to my mission. Are you committed to yours, Mr Chairman?'

– Former Portsmouth chairman, Milan Mandaric, recalled a letter he received from a soldier in Afghanistan who told him he 'went into battle wearing his Pompey shirt under his uniform'.

'I noticed fans carrying paraphernalia such as watermelons, loaves of bread, landline telephones, cabbages and giant dolls. In the frenzy and ecstatic cacophony after a team scores, a fan of the winning team will eat the cabbage or watermelon or take a bite from the giant loaf. This act sends a message to the competing team that "we shall eat you up".'

– South African football writer, Antony Kaminju, who 'embarked on a journey to find out who these [South African] fans are and what drives them to put on such elaborate performances'.

'For the most committed fans ... sport functions as a kind of surrogate religion; note the reverential attitudes of many fans toward their teams and their idolisation of particular players. It may even be that sport has grown in social significance because it now performs some of the functions assigned to religion in earlier societies.'

– Eric Dunning, author, 1996.

'They are taking the proverbial pee out of us loyal fans.'

– World-famous violinist and almost equally famous Aston Villa fan Nigel Kennedy was raging against his favourite club in a *Times* arts pages interview in August 2013, complaining, 'I am not going to renew my season ticket while they have this policy of grooming young players just to sell them on.'

'Thanks to whoever made the magnificent swan balloon hat for me! Marvellous work.'

– Tweet from Swannyg66, the Twitter name of England cricketer Graeme Swann, who wore a fan-created balloon hat made of white, orange and black balloons in the shape of a swan (when off-pitch) for the final two days of the dramatic final Ashes Test Match of 2013, which ended in a draw when the players were controversially taken off for bad light. He woke up the next morning having lost it and wondering who the fan who had created it was.

'The attending fan is our most important fan. We want the stadium full.'

– Premier League chief executive Richard Scudamore at the start of the 2013–14 season, apparently overlooking the fact that new regulations about the siting of TV cameras meant that sixty season-ticket holders (aka fans) at Old Trafford, up to twenty at Fulham, thirty at Arsenal, over 200 at Chelsea and a number of groups at Liverpool had either been moved or lost their places altogether.

'The prime age for sports fanaticism is about ten. Any younger, and you don't really know what's going on. Any older, and you've discovered the opposite sex, which may reshuffle your priorities for the next several decades.'

– American football writer Greg Hanlon, *New York Times*, 31 August 2013.

'They had absolutely no respect for the athletes. Kids would push each other in front of the race for a joke. On a climb, one spectator stole my sunglasses from my face while I was racing – I wasn't even out the back going slowly, I was right in the action.'

– Pro cyclist Charly Wegelius on riding in the Giro d'Italia, in his 2013 book *Domestique*.

BAD SHOT

After announcing that his Albanian club, Partizani Tirana, would be boycotting future league matches because of assaults by fans on players and officials, coach Perlat Musta was left in a coma after being shot in 1998.

AWAY BAN

Millwall fans upheld their reputation at an FA Cup quarter-final game in 1985 when they ripped plastic seats from their moorings and hurled them on the pitch at Kenilworth Road where their team were playing Luton Town. They then attacked the 200 police (injuring thirty-one) who were there for security purposes, forcing the referee to take players off the pitch for twenty-five minutes, leading ultimately to a ban on away fans at the ground.

DUMBED DOWN

When Queens Park beat Dumbarton 2–1 in the 1881 Scottish Cup final, the latter were awarded a replay on the grounds that 'the men had been interfered with by the crowd encroaching upon the space allotted for play'. The replay did nothing to help Dumbarton however: Queens Park won 3–1.

CROWD TROUBLE

A record British fan turn-out of 149,547 paid at Hampden Park to see Scotland play England in 1937 – but it is estimated that an additional 10,000 found a way into the ground without paying.

THE ROYAL ARSENAL?

The Sun reported in 2007 that the Queen had revealed that she was an Arsenal fan, having followed them since player Denis Compton had caught her attention. Also an accomplished cricketer, Compton made his debut for Arsenal in 1936.

DESPERATE MEASURES

In 1974, in an effort to stop the match, fans invaded the pitch in the eighty-second minute as Manchester City were 1–0 up on Man U, who faced relegation if they lost. Although the game was abandoned the result stood.

On the same date, 27 April, in 1996, Brighton fans invaded their own pitch, wrecked both goals, hurled wooden stakes into the crowd, tried to storm the players' tunnel and forced the abandonment of the Division Two match against York.

Fans were protesting at the decision by the club's directors to sell the Goldstone Ground, their home for ninety-four years, to a property company, and share the Fratton Park ground of Portsmouth FC, to pay off debts of £6 million.

CEREMONIAL SACRIFICE

In what most of us might regard as a slight overreaction, Chinese teenager Xia Qianli responded rather badly to being banned from watching the opening ceremony of the 1990 World Cup. He strangled his father.

GIANT CALL

During a National League game in 1949 between the Philadelphia Phillies and New York Giants, New York was ahead 3–2 in the ninth inning when umpire George Barr made a controversial call in NY's favour. The Philadelphia players complained, but the call was not reversed; Philadelphia fans then threw glass bottles onto the field, and the barrage continued despite pleas over the public address system. Umpire Al Barlick was hit in the back of the head by a tomato. After waiting for fifteen minutes, Barlick ruled the game by forfeit to the Giants.

JIM'LL FIX IT

'Is there a linesman in the house?' was the plea to fans as Arsenal prepared to take on Liverpool in a 1972 League game only for the flag-man, Denis Drewitt, to pull a muscle and drop out. Former Fulham player and TV pundit Jimmy Hill answered the call and duly took over on the line.

FANS SCORE IN GOALLESS DRAW

Pitch invasions by fans are relatively commonplace – but they usually happen during a game and aren't particularly intimate affairs.

However, in August 2013, two Danish fans were clearly so disappointed at the lack of goals during the match they had just watched that they decided they should give a demonstration of how simple it is to score.

They were photographed having sex on the very pitch where their team, Brøndby, had just played out a 0–0 bore-draw.

The couple were spotted under floodlights in the pitch's centre circle by security staff at Brøndby's Copenhagen ground following the goalless Danish Superliga match against Randers. A picture of the on-field action was posted on Twitter.

Brøndby spokesman Mikkel Davidsen posted on Twitter: 'Great match, but disappointed over the 0–0 and many missed chances. But the couple in the centre circle helps the mood.'

CAN-ARY YOU BELIEVE IT?

When Norwich fan Paul Murrell married wife Alison in 1986, their reception featured not a disco but commentary from the Canaries' vital league match against West Ham. The game ended in a 1–1 draw.

FEELING SHEEP-ISH

'It is great you brought a sheep for the Shakhter fans, although I don't think any of them would want to see this one killed. It's too cute for that.' Such were the words of sheepish fan Almaz Amirzhan, in Glasgow for Kazakhstan side Shakhter Karagandy's Champions League game against Celtic in August 2013, on learning that police had banned the fans' usual pre-match ritual slaughter of a lamb. Instead, the *Daily Record* presented fans with a toy version.

THE ANGRY ONE

Jose Mourinho was reportedly investigated by police in January 2013. His alleged offence? Kicking the backside of a fan who approached the then Real Madrid boss for a photograph when he was out shopping.

YOU WON'T WIN WITH KIDS

In 1972, FA Secretary Denis Follows came up with a master plan to beat the hooliganism that was rife within English football at the time. He demanded that they should 'ban all spectators aged under eighteen from the terraces'. Thankfully for the more youthful fans, his plan was widely ridiculed and dubbed 'Follows' Folly'.

FRAUDULENT FANS

Everton recorded an annual loss of £100,000 in 2001, reporting that the cause was adult fans using tickets at children's discounted prices.

ROOD BEHAVIOUR

After England fans booed their national team's lack-lustre performance at the 2010 World Cup against Algeria, striker Wayne Rooney reacted angrily to the cameras filming live after the final whistle had gone. He was reported to have said, 'Nice to see your home fans booing you. That's loyal supporters,' and received widespread condemnation for his comments. A year later Rooney was also criticised for his foul-mouthed and provocative celebrations after scoring a hat-trick away at West Ham.

IT EVENTUALLY CAUGHT ON...

The inaugural World Cup took place in 1930 in Uruguay. Now one of the biggest global sporting events, it was obviously less of a draw for fans in those early days: the first match between France and Mexico was watched by only 4,000 spectators in the Uruguayan capital of Montevideo. France won the contest 4–1.

REF WOUND UP

Referee Hugh Dallas needed stitches for a head wound after a coin was thrown at him by a spectator as Rangers beat Celtic 3–0 to clinch the Scottish title in an eventful 1999 game in which Dallas sent three players off.

CLARELY NAKED

Rugby fan Clare Morgan turned up to watch the match between Wales and Fiji in November 2002 wearing a jacket, boots and a Welsh flag draped around her as a skirt. Just after Wales scored their first try, she tore her clothes off and ran onto the Millennium Stadium pitch. Cheering fans rose to their feet as she held the flag aloft – before being tackled by a steward on the 22-metre line. The blonde from Swansea did it as a response to a challenge from her friends to raise £300 for the BBC's annual Children in Need Appeal. But her fund-raising streak landed her before Cardiff magistrates charged with breaching public order. Miss Morgan was conditionally discharged but was ordered to pay £55 costs.

A GREAT SEND-OFF

The iconic *Match of the Day* theme was played at an unusual venue in 1999 – at a memorial service in Newcastle for recently deceased fan Cardinal Basil Hulme.

HATS ON, LADIES

Buckingham Palace clamped down on unseemly fan behaviour in 1984, announcing that female racegoers would not be allowed into the Royal Enclosure at Ascot if 'their hats are too small'.

CELERY CAP

A bizarre chant by Chelsea fans involving references to celery culminated in incidents during the 2007 League Cup final when sticks of the vegetable were thrown at Arsenal's Cesc Fàbregas.

As a result, the inoffensive veg was banned from Stamford Bridge.

When top artist Mick Kirkbride was commissioned by Chelsea supporter Leon Deith to create a painting paying tribute to their followers, he included in it a supporter brandishing a stick of celery.

PERFECT EXIT

Giles Pellerin was such a superfan he even died at an American football match he had been watching. And not just any old game – it was his 797th consecutive USC college match, home and away. Giles, a former telephone company executive, died aged ninety-one on 21 November 1998. He was a University of Southern California Trojans supporter.

Y NOT USE THAT WORD?

An extraordinary row blew up after the FA warned Tottenham Hotspur fans to cease using the term 'Yid' in their chants or face the threat of criminal charges, as it was 'likely to be considered offensive by the reasonable observer' and was 'inappropriate in a football setting'.

However, the most common usage of the word had been by Spurs fans themselves, reclaiming it in an ironic way against its deployment by rival supporters in an anti-Semitic manner. Club fans protested that calling themselves the 'Yid Army' was a 'badge of pride'.

Prime Minister David Cameron took the fans' side, telling the *Jewish Chronicle* in September 2013 that 'there's a difference between Spurs fans describing themselves as Yids and someone calling someone a Yid as an insult'.

The Board of Deputies of British Jews reportedly believe the term should be banned, but this appeared to be a unique case of a group not wishing to have a term others believed to be offensive to them banned, in order that they could turn it back on their tormenters.

Commented the Tottenham Hotspur Supporters Trust: 'While we recognise that Spurs fans' use of the Y-word and associated identity may have caused some upset to members of the Jewish community, we sincerely believe no Spurs fan uses the term in a malicious way.'

Opined Spurs manager Andre Villas-Boas: 'I think our fans sing it with pride, it is something that they defend.'

Mail on Sunday sports writer Patrick Collins was in no doubt: 'To civilised people it [the Y-word] is a despicable slur which belongs to a more barbaric era.'

PITCH INVADER WAS HEARTILY 'ANDY

Stewards are trained to prevent fans running onto the pitch, so when two of them at White Hart Lane prevented a man from getting onto the pitch as a dramatic incident was unfolding it seemed an understandable reaction.

However, it could have been a fatal mistake.

Bolton Wanderers player Fabrice Muamba collapsed on the pitch during a match against Tottenham Hotspur on 17 March 2012.

He was clinically dead for some seventy-eight minutes.

But thanks in no small measure to the actions of Spurs fan and, in his working hours, consultant cardiologist Dr Andrew Deaner of the London Chest Hospital, he survived.

The drama was captured on camera. When the 23-year-old went down on the pitch for no apparent reason, Dr Deaner realised time was of the essence so decided to get onto the pitch to help, where a number of other medical specialists were also battling to save the player.

Initially his path to the pitch was barred by well-meaning stewards: 'Going down there were two young stewards who didn't want to know, but an older one let me through.'

The older one's reaction probably saved the player's life.

WHAT A CARD

Four-year-old Sam Livingstone was given a task at school in February 2012: 'Make a Valentine's Day card for your Mum.'

The youngster duly made a card – except that it was a 'Welcome to Newcastle' card for footballer Papiss Cisse, who had just joined the lad's favourite club, Newcastle FC.

His mum forgave him and helped him send the card to the football club.

When Cisse received the unexpected welcome, he was

so grateful that he went round to see the boy and his family to thank them.

'I couldn't believe my eyes when Dad told me and my brother Jack to go and see who was at the door. Papiss Cisse was standing there, that was amazing,' said Sam.

TRIGGER HAPPY

In 1976 Rigoberto Riasco of Panama won a split decision verdict over South Korean Yum Dong-Kyun in Korea.

After the decision had been announced, referee Larry Ronzilla inexplicably changed his score in favour of the Korean, who thus became WBC Super Bantamweight champ.

Returning home to America, Ronzilla explained the mystery of the revised decision: he had been persuaded to change his mind – by a gun-toting fan.

The title was handed back to rightful winner Riasco.

ROWDY CUSTOMERS

The first International Heavyweight Championship between John C. Heenan, US, and Tom Sayers, England, in 1860 had reached round thirty-seven when the referee fled from the ring to avoid assault at the hands of 'rowdies who tore the ropes and broke into the ring'.

Five referee-less rounds later, it was declared a draw.

MUM'S THE WORD

Rich Keeling thought he'd done the hard work when he poleaxed opponent Bill Redford during their 1952 welterweight bout in Louisville, only to find himself on the canvas within seconds – put there by a vicious right-hand by Redford's outraged mother.

ONE FINAL DISAPPOINTMENT

Lifelong Millwall fan Fred Swann died five years before Millwall reached Wembley for the 1999 League Trophy Final against Wigan, but family members bought him a ticket anyway – which they took to the match and put on the allocated seat. Fred 'saw' his team lose to a last-minute goal.

A MARROW VICTORY

Australian batsman Syd Gregory was used to winning trophies during his career at the turn of the twentieth century, but was left nonplussed during a game in Sydney in the 1908–09 season, when a fan made an impromptu trophy presentation to him.

A contemporary report explained how,

after a ten-minute delay on account of rain, the game was resumed. A man from the shilling portion of the ground climbed over the fence and walked to Gregory.

Reaching out his hand, he made an obeisance worthy of a Chinese Mandarin. Then he placed at Gregory's feet a huge vegetable marrow, remarking that the customs of various nations in prehistoric and later times was to do homage to heroes by making some small offering.

Gregory, who seemed unable to grasp the situation, handed back the trophy.

At this the donor looked offended, but he placed it behind the wicket where Gregory was batting, saying, 'While that remains there it will act as a talisman. You will score 1,000.'

Just then a policeman rushed forward, and the man was soon marched towards the gate.

U-INSANE BOLT?

Usain Bolt's memorable 2012 Olympic Games 100m final triumph could have been ruined by a fan of his chief rival, Yohan Blake, who hurled a bottle onto the track as the runners prepared for the race.

Ashley Gill-Webb, 34, of South Milford, North Yorkshire, was arrested at the Olympic Stadium on 5 August 2012.

Gill-Webb, who also shouted at athletes including Bolt, was found guilty of two public order offences at Stratford Magistrates' Court in January 2013.

His lawyers claimed he was suffering from a manic episode.

Gill-Webb was found guilty of intending to cause the 100m finalists harassment, alarm or distress by using threatening, abusive or disorderly behaviour – he shouted at Bolt, 'I want you to lose. Usain, you are bad, you are an a***hole.'

District Judge William Ashworth said:

The two charges relate to a period of two to three minutes before the start of the Olympic 100m men's final on 5 August 2012.

Mr Gill-Webb quite deliberately looked over his right shoulder and then turned round to look over his left shoulder to see if anyone was watching him and then stepped for concealment behind other spectators.

Satisfied that he was not under observation, he threw the bottle very close to the competitors, who were listening for the starting gun.

David Robinson, Deputy Chief Crown Prosecutor, said:

'I am sure that he was at that point weighing up the chances of being caught before throwing the bottle in an effort to disrupt the start of the race and put off Usain Bolt. I am sure, therefore, that he was at that point acting rationally and wrongly.'

The court heard that Gill-Webb, who has bipolar affective disorder, managed to get into the Olympic Park and the stadium using an old ticket.

He pushed his way through the crowd in the exclusive seating area near the starting line, from where he threw the plastic bottle.

He was then tackled by Dutch judo champion Edith Bosch after he threw the bottle, who said to him, 'Dude, are you crazy?' She had heard him say, 'Bolt, I want you to lose,' the court heard.

Other witnesses said he also shouted at other finalists, including Jamaican sprinter Blake and Justin Gatlin of the US. Student Farzin Mirshahi said she had heard him yell, 'Believe in Blake, no Usain.'

Gill-Webb did not give evidence at the trial and denied the offences. However, his DNA was later found on the bottle.

Following the verdict Mr Robinson, prosecuting, said:

> Gill-Webb's decision to throw a bottle onto the track at the men's 100m final was reckless and irresponsible. This incident came close to disrupting the most-watched event of the 2012 Olympic Games, which was broadcast to millions of people across the world and for which many athletes had trained for years.

In February 2013, Gill-Webb was sentenced to an eight-week community order.

WINGING IT

Somewhat overexcited Detroit ice hockey fans, brothers Pete and Jerry Cusimano, storeowners in Detroit's Eastern Market, decided to support their team, the Red Wings, on 15 April 1952 – by flinging an octopus onto the ice rink at Olympia Stadium.

Explains the Red Wings' own website: 'Each tentacle was symbolic of a win in the play-offs.'

Clearly inspired by the action, the Red Wings went on to win the prestigious Stanley Cup, following which triumph it became the done thing to hurl an octopus onto the ice during every Red Wings play-off game in the tournament.

Even when they moved to the Joe Louis Arena in 1979, the tradition went with them.

In 1996, a 50lb cephalopod was thrown onto the ice on the day of the Conference Finals, and the previous year one of 38lb – along with almost three dozen others – had arrived during the national anthem.

MY NAME IS RIO...

Rio Ferdinand was considering his future with Manchester United and pondering whether to sign a new contract with the club when a 'gang of hooded fans' turned up outside his house, telling him, 'We're the United boys, f***ing sign your contract.'

Ferdinand spoke about the incident for the first time in January 2013, recalling that he had been snapped by media photographers when, by chance, he had met up with Chelsea chief executive Peter Kenyon, sparking rumours that he might be planning to quit the Old Trafford club.

He told of how he'd answered the door to the gang:

> So I go to the side door and grab a big bit of wood,
> jump on the side of the wall and I'm just about to
> scream 'raaaah!' when I see there's a massive group of
> people, with hoodies and caps covering their faces. I just
> thought, 'I'm going to get served up in a moment, so go
> bananas and they'll think you're a nutter!'

When one of the gang had issued the threat, Rio told reporters, 'I was like, "What you talking about? I've only just started negotiating, what you worrying about?" One of the neighbours had called the police by then and they got off when they heard the sirens.'

He stayed.

Ferdinand's clearly a tolerant man: a Manchester City fan who threw a coin at him, cutting him above the eye, after a match at the Etihad won by United in 2012, escaped without punishment when the player decided to take no further action.

In a tweet about the incident, Ferdinand wrote: 'Whoever threw that coin, what a shot!'

WELL BREAD FAN?

An Italian fan robbed a Dutch tennis star, Mark Koevermans, of victory over home hero Alberto Mancini during the 1991 Italian Open.

The game was at a vital stage, with Koevermans a point away from match point, when a spectator suddenly lobbed a half-eaten ham sandwich onto the court.

Umpire Richard Ings called a let – a decision which sent Koevermans into an apoplexy of anger, from which he never recovered, enabling Mancini to go on and win the match.

In the second set, during a pause in play while Koevermans was rallying from a 4–2 deficit, another fan had tossed an apple onto the court. Koevermans picked it up and handed it to Ings in the umpire's chair. 'Keep it and eat it afterwards,' a fan shouted from the stands.

REAL DYNAMITE PLAYER

'Stupid, dumb, foolish, childlike' – just a few of the ways in which his lawyer endeavoured to explain New York Mets baseball star Vince Coleman's behaviour in 1993 when he threw an explosive device, reckoned to be the equivalent of a quarter of a stick of dynamite, into a group of autograph-hunting fans outside the Los Angeles Dodgers' stadium following their match.

He injured three people, two of them children.

Coleman was later handed a suspended sentence, placed on three years' probation and ordered to do 200 hours of community service.

The Mets traded him to the Royals after the incident, and Coleman became convinced other clubs were unwilling to touch him.

Coleman later maintained that the issue was trumped up by the media, and that fans were more than 30 feet away – 'from here to the batting cage', he said while standing in front of the Mariners' dugout – when he set off the explosive device, an M-100 that reportedly cost just $1.50.

Coleman also claimed that a civil suit filed by the family of two-year-old Amanda Santos was dropped, and there was never an out-of-court settlement.

'The media said that I threw it into a crowd,' Coleman said. 'That wasn't true.'

Oh, that's okay, then...

BLUE JAY WAY

Canadian baseball star Roberto Alomar of the Toronto Blue Jays was ordered off the field during a July 1995 game – because a female fan was about to attempt to murder him.

Alomar was called back to the bench after police told club officials that Ontario factory worker Tricia Miller, 31, was out to kill their key player.

'She came to Toronto with the sole purpose of murdering Mr Alomar and then killing herself with the revolver. The gun was loaded, cocked and ready to fire,' revealed a police statement after the would-be perp was apprehended in the nick of time.

Ms Miller was later sentenced to nine months in jail. Alomar hired personal security.

STABBED IN THE BACK

A tennis fan attempted to kill Monica Seles by stabbing her in the back with a knife on 30 April 1993.

Six thousand spectators were watching in Hamburg as nineteen-year-old Seles was leading Maggie Maleeva 6–4, 4–3 in their quarter-final match, and she was sitting in a courtside seat during a change of ends when the shocking attack took place.

Seles was rushed to hospital with a wound half an inch (1.5 cm) deep in her upper back. Doctors said her injuries were serious but not life-threatening.

Gunter Parche, a 39-year-old unemployed lathe operator, was convicted of the stabbing in October 1993. Parche was charged following the incident, but was not jailed because he was found to be psychologically abnormal, and was instead sentenced to two years' probation and psychological treatment.

He was described as a loner, whose obsession with seeing Steffi Graf regain the world no. 1 ranking prompted the attack.

It was over two years before Monica Seles returned to tennis competition. Her first tournament was the 1995 Canadian Open, which she won.

Her career never fully recovered from the incident.

THE BALLOON GOES UP...

The Harvard vs. Yale University American football game (often referred to as The Game), a high-profile contest dating back to 1875, was the target of an elaborate prank by fans of a rival university in 1982 when a large, black weather balloon painted with 'MIT' all around was inflated, seemingly from nowhere, in the middle of the field, at the 46-yard line, startling not only fans and players but also a commentator, who reported that a bomb had fallen onto the pitch and exploded, creating a large crater!

The legend 'MIT' was the trademark of Massachusetts Institute of Technology, which had a history of elaborate pranks or hacks, often aimed at rival learning establishments.

This prank was part of an operation that had been in the works since 1948, when the first attempt to create it was discovered and stopped.

The balloon was inflated by a freon-driven hydraulic press buried three feet below the ground, and was powered by a vacuum-cleaner motor.

Members of the MIT's 'Bomb Squad' planted the device a few days before the game, making eight trips to the stadium during the dead of night. One said, 'We did it for the fun of it.'

The students were confident that the explosion would cause no bodily harm since it contained only harmless freon, and courteously attached a note explaining how to properly clean it up.

A headline in the next morning's *Boston Herald* declared, 'MIT 1, HARVARD–YALE 0: TECH PRANKSTERS STEAL THE SHOW'.

... BUT SVEN'S BALLOON BURST

Sven-Göran Eriksson's Manchester City side crashed out of the FA Cup in January 2008 – beaten by a balloon thrown onto the pitch by one of their own fans prior to kick-off.

In the build-up to the opening goal of the game, the ball ran into a group of blue and white balloons in the goalmouth, leaving City's Michael Ball struggling to get the ball clear and allowing Sheffield United's Luton Shelton to nip in and score.

Bafflingly, City staff had been complaining about the balloons earlier – but keeper Joe Hart did not clear them out of his penalty box.

City lost the game 2–1.

DIFFERENT TYPE OF COACHING

With their side battling to win promotion to the top division in Argentina, sixty-six supporters who were heading for Chacarita Juniors' November 2008 away trip to fellow Buenos Aires side Talleres were desperate to get to the game on time.

So desperate, in fact, that they hijacked, at knife-point,

two city bus drivers to divert their vehicles from their normal route to take them to the game.

The drivers came up trumps and got their unexpected passengers (sixty-three men and three women) to the ground – where they still missed the game, by dint of being arrested on arrival.

It was some small compensation that Chacarita won the game 3–2 and went on to win promotion.

BY GEORGE, HE WAS THERE AGAIN...

Australian visitor to the 2012 London Olympics Robyn Glynn was there as a spectator and sports fan, but she brought a ghostly echo of the London Games of 1948 to the modern equivalent.

George Avery won a silver medal for Australia in the London Olympics of 1948, competing in the hop, step and jump, as the event was then known.

Once he knew that the 2012 Games were to be held in London, George, despite living in Sydney, was determined to return as a fan to the scene of his greatest success.

Amazingly, not only was George there, but he was also able to be part of the triple jump, as the event had since been renamed, at the London Olympics in 2012 – albeit he was dead by then!

'My father wanted to relive his second place at the 1948 Games by attending the 2012 Games. The whole family promised to bring him, but sadly he died in 2006 and was cremated,' George's daughter, Robyn Glynn, told Australia's *The Age* newspaper.

However, the rest of the family decided to go anyway, and to take George's ashes with us, so we could fulfil his final wish.

We had tickets for the finals of the triple jump and we managed to sneak his urn in past the officials. Actually, we did more than just sneak him in: we snuck ourselves down to the edge of the track, took off the lid, and in the breeze we let his ashes go.

Off he went, through the air and right over the triple jump run-up.

We'd all decided that was where Dad would have wanted to come back to, and there he still is, all over the run-up and in the pit. He'd really wanted to be there in person, and this was the next best thing.

KEEPING MUM

Two promising British light heavyweights were matched against each other in September 1989.

Tony Wilson had twice won national titles at the weight as an amateur and had gone on to do likewise as a pro, but the unbeaten Steve McCarthy had managed to gain the upper hand, having floored Wilson in the third round.

The fight was clearly going McCarthy's way and Wilson found himself taking heavy punishment while penned into a corner.

The raucous crowd urged on their favourite, but one Wilson fan in particular was finding it hard to watch the former champ getting the worst of the battle – so she leaped out of her seat and climbed up onto the apron of the ring, where she removed one of her stylish high-heeled shoes and used it to set about McCarthy's cranium.

In the confusion, McCarthy clearly thought the fight had been stopped and turned away to celebrate – only to be targeted again by the fiery female who, fortunately, was prevented from getting at him.

It was Wilson's mother, Minna, and she eventually had to be forcibly restrained and removed from the ring – having left her mark, literally, on McCarthy, who was complaining of a cut head and who now refused to resume the fight.

As a result, the referee, Adrian Morgan, disqualified McCarthy and awarded the bout to Wilson by a technical knockout.

That verdict was eventually appealed but, bizarrely enough, was upheld by the British Boxing Board of Control, which said it would honour the referee's final decision despite 'the unsatisfactory nature of the ending of this contest'. However, they also ordered a rematch – which never happened – from which Minna Wilson would be barred.

Wilson's career collapsed after this and he won only three of ten more fights, while McCarthy went on to win the British title but made little further progress.

BOAT RACE'S SINKING FEELING

Trenton Oldfield decided that it would be a good idea to take a swim in the Thames – a baffling enough decision at the best of times, but doubly so given that he chose to go for a dip at precisely the same time as the crews were battling it out to win the 2012 Oxford vs. Cambridge Boat Race.

As a result the crews had to stop rowing out of fear that they might injure him.

So Trenton didn't exactly get a rapturous welcome from crews or spectators while making what he later claimed was 'a protest against elitism'.

It looked more like a bloke trying to grab hold of an oar to avoid drowning, to be honest.

Later in the year, the 36-year-old Australian, who had lived in Britain since 2001, pleaded not guilty but was found to have caused a public nuisance, and was sentenced to six months, ordered to pay £750 costs, and told by judge Anne Molyneux, 'No good ever comes from prejudice.'

According to media reports, Oldfield 'smirked' as the judge also called his actions 'deliberate, disproportionate and dangerous', adding, 'You made your decision to sabotage the race based on the membership or perceived membership of its participants of a group to which you took exception. That is prejudice.'

And she skewered his justification for his actions by pointing out: 'You did nothing to address inequality by giving yourself the right to spoil the enjoyment of others.'

Oldfield claimed he was protesting because the race was a 'symbol of a lot of issues in Britain around class

– 70 per cent of (the) government pushing through very significant cuts are Oxford or Cambridge graduates'.

He added, 'I don't have any regrets with what I did. Lots of people thought it made it the most exciting Boat Race ever.'

Matthew Pinsent did not concur with that opinion. The four-time Olympic champion had raised the alarm:

> I looked up the river and saw ahead what appeared to be a balloon. After a few seconds I noticed what I recognised to be a human arm in the water. I began rapid discussions with the race umpire to change the course. The risk for the swimmer was great – he could have been killed if he had been struck by an oar or the rigging, which is metal.
>
> The police came to see me that night and took a statement, which took me by surprise: it wasn't clear to me what they were going to charge the swimmer with. People said, 'I hope it doesn't happen at the Olympics,' but I'd always reply, 'Look, I want to live in a country where protest is possible.' However unwelcome it was, I still value the freedom to do that.

Oldfield eventually served seven weeks of his sentence and declared on release that he would be prepared to take similar action in the future.

The race itself was ultimately restarted but the contest was again ended prematurely when Oxford broke an oar in a clash, allowing the Cambridge crew to row to victory.

In his *Daily Mail* column, former *Sun* editor Kelvin Mackenzie made a suggestion that 'Oxford and Cambridge drop the oars and use powerboats so that if an "anti-elitist" protestor pops up in the Thames they won't be able to stop in time. That would be a sadness, wouldn't it?'

When the 2013 Boat Race took place it was with a detachment of Royal Marines in a string of inflatable boats lying in wait in case of any attempted waterborne interruption of proceedings. There was none. Amazingly, Oldfield, who was later threatened with deportation, claimed police wrote to him to say they were 'keen to facilitate any peaceful protest'. He responded, 'I'll probably have a ramble across the Cotswolds instead.'

LONE FAN RAISES GLASS TO AWAY VICTORY

After Udinese beat Sampdoria 2–0 in an away Serie A match in December 2012, the victorious Udinese players dedicated their victory to fan Arrigo Brovedani – because he was the only supporter who bothered to turn up to see his team win the game!

Although Udinese are one of the smaller teams in the division and seldom take large quantities of fans to away games, and even allowing for the cold-weather snap at the time, this was a unique occasion – even to the extent that the home side's stewards bought him coffee and home supporters invited him for a drink after the game.

Brovedani, a 37-year-old wine merchant, was somewhat bemused.

> I went there thinking I'd find five or six other people. I went into the stadium while Udinese were warming up – I shouted and said 'hi' to the team. When I went in the local fans booed me. I felt a bit offended – but in the end they clapped and invited me for coffee and a meal, and the club managers gave me a shirt – they wished me a Merry Christmas.

Genoa, where Sampdoria play, is a marathon 600-mile round-trip drive from Udinese's Friuli base, and Mr Brovedani had coupled a business appointment there with watching the game.

After the game he discovered his team had dedicated their win to him and asked him along as a special guest to their next home match.

DEVIL OF A FAN

'There are riders who change their side of the road when seeing me. I don't know why they do so, but I take it as a sign not to chase them. Especially some riders of the female peloton do so.'

Since 1993, when he first pitched up at the Tour de France, Dieter 'Didi' Senft has been known as the Tour de France and Giro d'Italia 'Devil', or El Diablo.

With his bushy beard making him even more photogenic, the German fan has become a familiar sight, much beloved of TV producers and media photographers, at the Tour's and Giro's many stages, wearing his red devil costume and painting trident symbols on the road.

He does often manage to get too close to riders for their comfort, but claims he never has any intention of impeding them.

Senft has attributed the inspiration for his costume to a German cycling announcer Herbert Watterot, who once called the last lap of local cycling races 'the Red Devil's Lap'.

Another explanation for the nickname is that Didi adopted it in tribute to his favourite rider, Italian Claudio Chiappucci, nicknamed 'El Diablo' by Spanish fans – a soubriquet that stuck with him for the rest of his career.

Didi told an interviewer in 2004:

> When the advertising caravan arrives, I jump on all the vehicles, I chase the caravan girls and I scream at them. When the riders are passing by, I never afflict them. It's a question of respect for them. I chase them for the media, only from behind and never too close.

The German is also an inventor who has created over 100 bicycles, including the largest in the world, and earned a listing in the *Guinness Book of Records* for building the largest mobile guitar, taking the form of a bicycle. He also runs a bicycle museum.

During the 2006 Tour of Switzerland, Didi painted his signature trident on the road the day before the competitors came by. But Swiss police arrived, told him it was illegal and that he must either pay a fine or go to jail. He was also forced to remove the painting from the road. Also in 2006, the Devil encountered the 'Specialised Angel' at the Giro d'Italia in 2006. The winged, scantily clad blonde's role was created as a publicity stunt by a bike company to play off against the notoriety of the Tour Devil.

Didi reckons he has a couple of dozen tridents made of various materials, including aluminium and plastic;

the latter is apparently the only type he is allowed to carry when he travels by plane.

Not everyone is a fan of this fan, however, and in 2010 website atwistedspoke.com commented of him, 'The Devil has some personal hygiene issues so it's just another reason not to go to Hell. His feet are filthy and the costume definitely has too much mileage on it.'

In 2003, Tour writer Les Woodland called him 'an annoyance at whom riders throw bottles and other rubbish if they get the chance'.

And in 2006, *Bicycling* magazine writer Bill Strickland described him as 'a quirky, sometimes cranky and often smelly superfan' while being somewhat more appreciative of the Specialised Angel!

Didi's attendance record at the Tour was interrupted in 2012 when, now aged sixty, he had to undergo brain surgery, but he returned at the 2013 event, predicting that he had another twenty tours in him.

THE GRAND PRIEST

Laicised – or defrocked – Irish Roman Catholic priest Cornelius 'Neil' Horan, sometimes referred to as The Grand Prix Priest or The Dancing Priest, became notorious for disrupting sports events in order to promote his religious belief that the end of the world is nigh.

Horan began his programme of interference at the British Grand Prix on 20 July 2003, when he ran across the track at Silverstone Circuit, wearing a kilt and carrying a banner reading, 'Read the Bible. The Bible is always right.'

With cars swerving around him and the safety car on its way, Horan was tackled by a race marshal and arrested. He was charged with, and pleaded guilty to, aggravated trespass and sentenced to two months' imprisonment.

The faith was strong, however, and the following year Horan was spotted by police at the Epsom Derby. Believing that he was about to run in front of the horses, the police tackled him to the ground. He was later released without charge.

Nor was he deterred by the high security surrounding the 2004 Athens Olympics amid fears of a terrorist attack: on 29 August Horan ran onto the course of the men's marathon event near the 35km mark, carrying a placard reading: 'The Grand Prix priest. Israel fulfilment of prophecy says the Bible, the second coming is near.'

Where Greek security had failed, however, the Greek public prevailed: after Horan pushed Brazilian Vanderlei de Lima, who was leading the race, into the crowds alongside the course, he found himself being hauled off the shaken runner by a Greek spectator.

Polyvios Kossivas subdued Horan and helped de Lima up before the police arrived on the scene. Following the encounter with Horan, de Lima suffered from leg cramps and muscle pain, and although he continued running and completed the race, he was pushed back into third place after being passed by Italian Stefano Baldini and American Mebrahtom Keflezighi. De Lima later reportedly commented:

It was crazy on the course, it was bad. For me it's very, very bad.

I was scared, because I didn't know what could happen to me, whether he was armed with a knife, a revolver or something and whether he was going to kill me … That's what cost me the gold medal.

The Brazilian Track Federation launched an appeal, seeking a gold medal for de Lima, but it was denied.

Horan was handed a suspended sentence of a year by a Greek court and fined €3,000. The judge gave him a suspended sentence on account of his mental state. Horan also apologised.

Horan's brother, Dan, reportedly later apologised for his brother's actions and argued that he should have been jailed: 'The family are totally shocked and appalled by what he is doing.'

On 20 January 2005, Horan was formally defrocked by the Catholic Church. Horan was quoted as saying, 'I completely reject this decision ... I appeal to the much higher court of Heaven and the court of Jesus Christ.'

Horan went on, bizarrely, to appear on *Britain's Got Talent* in May 2009. He danced a soft jig on the show, received a standing ovation from the audience, and was put through to the next round. He did not make the live semi-finals.

MY WINNING STREAK

If I'm honest, I'd rather hoped it would happen. So it didn't much upset me when my master plan came together, despite a few critical comments appearing in the media.

When William Hill became the first and, until now, the only bookmakers ever to operate a betting facility at the Wimbledon Championships back in the mid-1970s, it had produced a huge amount of controversy and media coverage, as well as a substantial betting turnover.

One of the spin-offs of that undertaking was that I continued to look for ways to associate William Hill betting odds with the tournament – offering prices about what the weather might do during the fortnight, whether Cliff Richard would burst into song when play halted because of a downpour and, most deviously of all, about whether Wimbledon would ever fall victim to the antics of a Centre Court streaker.

I thought that if I put out the odds, some bright spark of a tennis fan cum self-publicist might realise that they would be in a position to put a bet on it happening and then make it a self-fulfilling prophecy/winning bet by performing the streak themselves.

I do admit I thought it would be a bloke who'd try it, so when it did finally happen in 1996 I was somewhat surprised that the perpetrator was a woman.

But while 23-year-old Melissa Johnson, a student who was working in one of the catering facilities at the tournament, might well have added to her wages from the proceeds of a bet at the 4/1 I was offering through my company, she could not have realised that her action may well have cost one of the finalists all chance of winning the most prestigious prize in tennis.

For Ms Johnson performed her streak in front of 14,000 spectators and a collection of Royals (who *were* amused), even as finalists Richard Krajicek and MaliVai Washington were warming up for the final, leaping over a barrier and running the length of the court wearing a face-splitting smile and a tiny apron to protect at least a smidgeon of her modesty.

Both players failed to resist the temptation of copping an eyeful, and Washington paid his own tribute by lifting his shirt to show off his own bare torso, but then crashed to a straight-sets defeat in just over ninety minutes, after which he commented, 'I look over and see this streaker. She lifted up the apron and, gee, she was smiling at me. I got flustered and three sets later I was gone.'

Even the normally strait-laced All England Club remarked that the streak 'did at least provide some light amusement for our loyal and patient supporters, who have had a trying time during the recent bad weather'.

I authorised payment of winning streaker bets with a wry grin – and, yes, you can still have the same bet for the next Wimbledon if you like...

COURIER WINS IN A FLASH

Jim Courier was seventh seed at the 1994 French Open, a tournament he had won in both 1991 and 1992, and in which he had been the beaten finalist in 1993.

But, popular though he was at the event, Courier was taking on home contender Jean-Philippe Fleurian in the first round, and wasn't expecting to be the darling of the French supporters.

Not allowing the domestic fans to distract him, Courier breezed through the first set 6–1.

Once the second set got under way, however, Courier suddenly seemed to find it difficult to concentrate – and served an unprecedented seven consecutive faults.

It was all he could do to keep the ball in play against his unheralded opponent, but his professionalism finally saw him through to 6–4 second- and third-set margins to make it through to round two.

Only after the match did it emerge what a unique obstacle had been placed in the way of Courier's progress, by a shameless and partisan female fan.

It was reported by *The Times* that 'Courier's concentration had been broken by the activities of a female who was seen occasionally to give him a shout, upon which she would part her legs, raise her skirt and show her knickers!'

Apparently her brazen effort to distract the American had been noticed by officials, and stewards had moved in to put an end to the flashy displays, telling her, in effect, 'You're (k)nicked, Mademoiselle.'

It was, however, later alleged that *The Times*'s version of events had been somewhat cleaned up as, in fact, the spectator's actions were more akin to those portrayed by Sharon Stone in the most famous scene from the movie *Basic Instinct*.

Mr Courier kept quiet about the more intimate details of the, er, bare-faced attempt to prevent him from keeping his mind on the job in hand, but maybe he was still thinking about her when he was beaten in the semi-final by the eventual tournament winner, Spaniard Sergi Bruguera.

YOU CANT GET AWAY WITH THAT

No player did more than Eric Cantona to help the Premiership capture headlines in its early years.

But for all his skill and high-profile on-pitch arrogance, his most famous kick in English football was the two-footed one he ran across the pitch to leap and aim at the midriff of shocked Crystal Palace fan Matthew Simmons, who had been loudly abusing the Man U legend, who had just been sent off in a 1995 Premiership match for kicking Palace's Richard Shaw.

As the still fuming Frenchman walked towards the tunnel, Simmons came down from the stands and shouted at him, prompting Cantona's extraordinary, violent reaction.

Cantona, who later claimed he had been racially abused and that Simmons had thrown a missile at him, was banned for eight months and fined a total of £30,000. He was also sentenced to two weeks in prison, which was reduced to 120 hours' community service for the attack. Simmons was later fined £500 for threatening language and behaviour.

United failed to win the title, and the phrase which he subsequently used while trying to explain his actions, 'When the seagulls follow the trawler, it's because they think sardines will be thrown into the sea', has been puzzling people ever since.

Sir Alex Ferguson later said, 'Over the years since then I have never been able to elicit an explanation of the episode from Eric, but my own feeling is that anger at himself over the ordering-off and resentment of the referee's earlier inaction combined to take him over the brink.'

Cantona was later asked on BBC's *Football Focus* what the highlight of his career was, responding, 'When I did the kung fu kick on the hooligan, because these kind of people don't have to be at the game. I think maybe it's like a dream for some, you know, sometimes to kick these kind of people.'

Another example of Palace manners happened in 1942 when, continuously barracked and pilloried by Crystal

Palace fans during a Football League South match, Spurs player Andy Duncan was so unnerved that he walked off the pitch – never to play for the club again.

FALDO NICKED IT

Coming to the sixteenth hole at Wentworth in the 1983 World Match Play tournament, Britain's Nick Faldo and Australia's Graham Marsh were level with three to play.

Faldo hit an approach shot which arrived on the green and sailed on into the spectators clustered around the hole.

Within seconds, appearing to defy the laws of physics, and without the knowledge of either Faldo or Marsh, who were both out of sight of the goings-on, Faldo's ball reappeared from the watching fans, heading back towards a decent landing place on the green.

The Times's golfing correspondent John Hennessy would later refer to this 'appalling piece of dishonesty on the part of some baboon in the crowd'.

However, the match referee had also been unsighted and, despite conferring with a greenside official, decided that Faldo could go ahead and play the ball where it had ended up.

The referee said it had been 'a rub of the green', a decision which the sporting Marsh did not quibble with.

Faldo duly holed out in two putts for a four, leaving Marsh with a tricky three-footer to halve the hole.

Rather than concede the putt, Faldo, who was later criticised by the media, opted to make Marsh putt out – which he did, only to miss and lose the hole. Faldo went on to take the next hole and the match.

He eventually reached the final, where he was beaten by Greg Norman, amid allegations that the amazing, rebounding ball had been helped on its way by a punter who had bet on Faldo. That allegation smacks of an attempt to deflect blame for the situation and its aftermath by the referee and Faldo himself.

Aussie newspaper *The Age*'s golf correspondent, Trevor Grant, was blunt, later writing, 'People still want to question his (Faldo's) behaviour ... when a spectator threw his ball back onto the green.'

And US golfer David Graham declared in *Golf Digest* magazine, 'I don't think Faldo should have expected to reap the rewards for what some idiot did.'

Unrepentant Faldo insisted that 'two wrongs don't make a right' and added, 'On that green I asked Graham Marsh if he thought the ruling was OK and he answered "yes".'

The guilty fan – one of Faldo's or not – was never identified.

ASHEN-FACED FAN

The dying wish of a fan of Spanish club Real Betis was to continue supporting his team – even from beyond the grave.

Rather than simply sprinkle his father's ashes around the ground, his grieving son decided firstly to renew his dad's season ticket and club membership – and then to take him along to home matches in a glass urn.

This seemed, inexplicably, to upset the club's security stewards, it was revealed in November 1995, when officials suggested that the fan should leave his father's ashes in the trophy room.

But this suggestion in turn did not play well with cleaning staff, who objected to the 'morbid atmosphere' (well, a Spanish-language equivalent of such a phrase) it would create.

So a compromise was reached permitting the son to bring the father to games in a cardboard container described, again in Spanish, as 'a sort of milk carton' – which was placed on his seat in order to allow a clear view of the action.

'Every time Betis scores,' said the anonymous son poignantly, 'I give my dad a little shake.'

That would be a milkshake, presumably!

STAN-LEY KNIFE

Stan Walker went to a baseball game in Morristown, Ohio, in 1902.

A keen fan, he asked another spectator sitting alongside him if he could borrow his penknife in order to sharpen the pencil with which he intended to jot down details of the game as it unfolded.

Willingly, the neighbour handed the knife over.

As Walker took the knife from him a foul ball was hit hard in his direction, striking him on the hand now clutching the knife, and driving the blade fatally into his chest.

NAKED TRUTH ABOUT FANS

At the tender age of twenty-five, Australian Michael O'Brien was credited with being the first modern-day streaker at a major sporting event when, on 20 April 1974, he ran out naked onto the ground of an England vs. France rugby union match at Twickenham.

O'Brien was captured by a policeman, PC Bruce Perry, who covered the streaker's genitals with his police helmet. A photograph of O'Brien under arrest became one of the most reproduced and iconic shots of a streaker. O'Brien, long-haired, bearded and naked in front of a jeering and cheering crowd, is surrounded and supported by cops as he is arrested. The policeman's helmet – calm down – later went on display in the museum at Twickenham.

That same year, Randwick racecourse in Sydney, Australia, witnessed a streakers' race, although this one wasn't scheduled and anticipated – well, only by two people, a man and a woman.

It took place while the Doncaster Stakes was being run. 'Streakers hit Royal Randwick', wrote Roy Higgins – who trained the winner, Tontonan – in his autobiography, *The Professor*.

The bizarre part about it was that the streakers did it while the race was being run. As soon as the field had set off, they came onto the track near the 100m mark and staged their own race down to the winning post, absolutely starkers. 'One erstwhile photographer, Ron Bickley, snapped the streakers in action and, without being crude, you might say they were both very well endowed,' Higgins reported.

He added: 'The photographer inset the snap of the streakers into a corner of the picture of Tontonan beating Toltrice, and copies are collectors' items. And the caption tells the story. It says: "The colt won by a good length."'

In 1975 Merchant Navy cook Michael Angelow had gone to Lord's to see England play Australia in the Ashes series when he was bet by a friend that he wouldn't streak onto the pitch. So he did, becoming the first to do such a thing at that venue, albeit still quaintly wearing trainers and socks. He not only ran onto the playing track but vaulted over the stumps, creating a memorable photographic image which appeared in most of the next day's papers.

Legendary commentator John Arlott was on duty:

> We have got a freaker [*sic*] down the wicket now, not very shapely as it is masculine and I would think it has seen the last of its cricket for the day. The police are mustered, so are the cameramen and Greg Chappell. No! He has had his load, he is being embraced by a blond policeman and this may be his last public appearance. But what a splendid one.

Having been arrested, Angelow pleaded guilty to a charge of outraging public decency and was duly fined £20 – the amount he had won for winning the bet.

Australian player Doug Walters commented, 'You didn't expect that kind of behaviour in England, certainly not in those days and at Lord's of all places.'

Angelow did not enjoy the aftermath of his actions: 'I

was offered money to do it again at the Grand National and Wimbledon, but I didn't want to know. I also had people offering me parts in porn movies and all sorts of weirdos calling me.'

However, the true Queen of Streakers is always going to be Erika (sometimes known as Erica) Roe. As I explained in the introduction to this book, I was at Twickenham on the day in 1982 when the 24-year-old Petersfield art dealer's assistant threw off her inhibitions at half-time in a match in which England were leading bitter rivals Australia by six points to three.

England's skipper Bill Beaumont can never discuss his side's ultimate 15–11 victory without recalling the moment at which he became aware of Erika's exploits, as he was in the middle of endeavouring to inspire the players with his inspirational pitchside interval speech, only to become aware that no one was listening.

'What's up?' he demanded to know, and one of the players explained, 'Everyone's watching that girl over there who seems to have your bum on her chest, Bill.'

Erika had deliberately chosen half-time to launch her unforgettable intrusion as she 'didn't want to interrupt the game'.

'Titters at Twickers' was just one of the headlines to result from Roe's arrival on the pitch, not only flaunting her more-than-ample upper-body charms, but also, incredibly, puffing away on a cigarette, while remaining fully clad in a pair of jeans from the waist down, thus not strictly speaking fully embracing the true streaking experience.

Erika told the *Observer* newspaper:

I blame my elder sister Sally, who was going with a clutch of rugger-bugger friends and roped me in. About twenty-five of us arrived and went straight to the beer tent, where we spent quite some time. I was definitely tipsy. I couldn't do anything so ridiculous as streaking cold-blooded!

One of the guys in our group had the hots for me and kept getting too close for comfort, so my friend Sarah Bennett and I moved down to the front. We were getting a bit bored, thought we should do something and within seconds had decided 'let's streak'. It was an impulse thing. We threw our clothes off. I handed my bra to some people behind me – and my packet of Marlboro. Half-time arrived, and off I went.

I remember running like hell, knowing I was being pursued and looking back for Sarah, who didn't join me. I heard all this screaming and thought, 'I have to get off, the second half is starting.' But I quickly realised the roar was for me. Then of course I behaved like an egotistical bitch, put my arms in the air and went, 'Yes! Hi!' That was fun. Then I turned back to try and get Sarah out, which is why I was caught.

In the three years afterwards, when I did personal appearances and opened shops, I only made about £8,000. The streak was a strange lesson and I'm glad I did it. It has made me a better person and more content because people have this illusion that being famous is incredible, which it is – but only if you're famous for doing something worthwhile. I became famous, but only for my boobs.

FAN MAN

James Jarrett Miller became known as Fan Man when he interrupted a major sporting event in a genuinely unique and unprecedented manner which stunned and staggered those present and those watching on TV.

Miller was a parachutist and paraglider pilot from Henderson, Nevada. The stunt which brought him to prominence took place at the 6 November 1993 world title fight between Evander Holyfield and Riddick Bowe at Caesars Palace on the Las Vegas Strip.

'Fan Man' made headlines when he used his powered paraglider to fly into the arena, eventually crashing into the ring to the total bemusement of the gobsmacked heavyweights.

Miller descended into the arena in the second minute

of the seventh round of the fight, after circling Caesars Palace for ten minutes. The lines of his paraglider became caught up in the overhead lights. He landed on the top rope of the ring with his parachute still tangled in the lights. He tried to hang on with one foot and one hand on the top rope for a few seconds, but fell or was perhaps dragged into the crowd by spectators, his parachute ripping away as he tumbled.

Fans and security men swarmed around him immediately – then began attacking him. Miller was knocked unconscious during the attack, and was rushed to hospital as spectators cut his paraglider into pieces for souvenirs. He was later charged with 'dangerous flying' and released on $200 bail.

Miller later claimed his ring crash was accidental, declaring that it was caused by mechanical problems, but TV footage suggests Miller's descent towards the ring area was carefully planned.

'It was a heavyweight fight,' Miller would joke ruefully, 'but I was the only guy who got knocked out.'

Miller took his nickname from the paramotor, a lightweight engine and propeller attached to his harness.

He obviously valued his notoriety and he would hit the headlines again.

In January 1994, Miller flew into a Denver Broncos– Los Angeles Raiders NFL football game at the Coliseum in Los Angeles and was promptly arrested for interfering with a sporting event.

A month later he turned up in England, skydiving into a Bolton Wanderers–Arsenal Premier League soccer match at Burnden Park.

Things became seriously weird when, in February of that year, Miller paraglided onto the roof of Buckingham Palace. He was painted green, with his private parts revealed as being covered in glow-in-the-dark paint when his trousers were removed.

He was accused of being a terrorist, slung in jail and deported.

His story ended in tragedy. Miller was reported missing on 22 September 2002. On 9 March 2003, a group of hunters bushwhacking through the woods on the Kenai Peninsula, Alaska, found a decomposing body, identified as that of Miller.

Police said he had chosen the remote Resurrection Pass Trail in Chugach National Forest, veering deep off-trail to a spot that might not have been discovered for years, if ever. Miller had hanged himself from a tree, reportedly using his parachute cords, and the death was ruled a suicide. Miller had been suffering from a debilitating heart disease and was overwhelmed by medical bills.

He left behind a pregnant girlfriend who, poignantly, had given birth to a son, Logan, on 14 February 2003.

BIBLIOGRAPHY

David Rayvern Allen, *Cricket Extras* (London: Guinness Books, 1988).

John Bryant, *The London Marathon* (London: Hutchinson, 2005).

Richard Cashman, David Headon and Graeme Kinross-Smith, *Australian Sporting Anecdotes* (South Melbourne: Oxford University Press Australia, 1993).

Jimmy Connors, *The Outsider* (London: Bantam Press, 2013).

Rhys Davis, *Book of Snooker Disasters & Bizarre Records* (London: Stanley Paul, 1986).

Robert Edelman, *Serious Fun* (Oxford: Oxford University Press, 1993).

Graham Edge and Keith Walmsley, *Sports Facts 1980* (London: Macdonald and Jane's, 1980).

Matthew Engel and Ian Morrison, *Sportspages Almanac 1991* (Farnham: Sportspages, 1990).

Matthew Engel and Ian Morrison, *Sportspages Almanac 1992* (Farnham: Sportspages, 1991).

Stan Greenberg, *Running Shorts* (London: Guinness Books, 1993).

Dan Gutman, *Baseball Babylon* (London: Penguin, 1992).

Freda Heywood, Malcolm Heywood and Brian Heywood, *Cloth Caps & Cricket Crazy* (Todmorden: Upper Calder Valley Publications, 2004).

David Hopps, *A Century of Great Cricket Quotes* (London: Robson Press, 1998).

Mike Huggins and Jack Williams, *Sport and the English 1918–1939* (London: Routledge, 2006).

Brian Hunt, *Northern Goalfields* (Northern League, 2000).

Graeme Kent, *Boxing Shorts* (London: Guinness Books, 1992).

David Levinson and Karen Christenson, *Encyclopedia of World Sport* (Santa Barbara: ABC-CLIO, 1996).

Desmond Lynam and David Teasdale, *The Sporting Word* (London: BBC Books, 1994).

James Montague, *When Friday Comes* (London: deCoubertin Books, 2013).

Geoffrey Moorhouse, *A People's Game* (London: Hodder & Stoughton, 1995).

Ian Morrison, *Radio Times Book of Sporting Dates* (London: BBC Books, 1993).

Peter Nichols, *Sports Yearbook 1997* (Brighton: Oddball, 1996).

Peter Nichols, *Sports Yearbook 1998* (Brighton: Oddball, 1997).

Peter Nichols, *Sports Yearbook 1999* (Brighton: Oddball, 1999).

Peter Nichols, *Sports Yearbook 2001* (Brighton: Oddball 2001).

Jeff Parietti, *The Book of Truly Stupid Sports Quotes* (London: Harper Perennial, 1995).

David Pickering, *Great Sporting Quotations* (York: Past Times, 2001).

Andrew Postman and Larry Stone, *The Ultimate Book of Sports Lists* (London: Bantam Books, 1990).

Simon Rae, *It's Not Cricket* (London: Faber and Faber, 2001).

George Raynor, *Football Ambassador at Large* (London: Sportsman's Book Club, 1960).

Tom Stenner, *Sport for the Million* (London: Sportsman's Book Club, 1959).

Geoff Tibballs, *Great Sporting Eccentrics* (London: Robson Press, 1997).

Geoff Tibballs, *Motor-Racing's Strangest Races* (London: Robson Press, 2001).

Wray Vamplew, Katharine Moore, John O'Hara, Richard Cashman and Ian F. Jobling, *The Oxford Companion to Australian Sport* (Oxford: Oxford University Press, 1992).

David Wallechinsky, *Complete Book of the Olympics* (London: Aurum Press, 1996).

David Wallechinsky, *Complete Book of the Winter Olympics* (London: Aurum Press, 2001).

D. L. Wann, M. J. Melnich, G. W. Russell and D. G. Pease, *Sports Fans: The Psychology and Social Impact of Spectators* (London: Routledge, 2001).

Les Woodland, *Yellow Jersey Companion to the Tour de France* (London: Yellow Jersey Press, 2003).